CORBAN
C O L L E G E

WITHDRAWN

LITERATURE-BASED READING

Children's Books and Activities to Enrich the K-5 Curriculum

by Mildred Knight Laughlin
and
Claudia Lisman Swisher

ORYX PRESS
1990

The rare Arabian Oryx is believed to have inspired the myth of the unicorn. This desert antelope became virtually extinct in the early 1960s. At that time several groups of international conservationists arranged to have 9 animals sent to the Phoenix Zoo to be the nucleus of a captive breeding herd. Today the Oryx population is nearly 800, and over 400 have been returned to reserves in the Middle East.

Copyright © 1990 by The Oryx Press
4041 North Central at Indian School Road
Phoenix, AZ 85012

Published simultaneously in Canada

Printed and Bound in the United States of America

∞ The paper used in this publication meets the minimum requirements of American National Standard for Information Science—Permanence of Paper for Printed Library Materials, ANSI Z39.48, 1984.

Library of Congress Cataloging-in-Publication Data

Laughlin, Mildred.
    Literature-based reading : children's books and activities to enrich the K–5 curriculum / by Mildred Knight Laughlin and Claudia Lisman Swisher.
        p.   cm.
    Includes bibliographic references.
    ISBN 0-89774-562-0
    1. Reading—Language experience approach.   2. Children—Books and reading.   3. Activity programs in education.   I. Swisher, Claudia Lisman.   II. Title.
LB1050.35.L38 1990
372.4—dc20   90-36415
                                                                              CIP

86641

Contents

Acknowledgment

Grateful acknowledgment is made to Desiree Webber, Mildred Laughlin's teaching assistant. Without her assistance in locating, delivering and returning books, and in typing copy, this work could not have been completed.

Introduction: Why Use Children's Literature to Teach Reading?

Regardless of the approach they prefer to teach reading, educators in recent years have used more children's literature than in the past to enrich the reading program. Two of the strongest reading approaches to date, the basal series and the whole language method, have integrated literature into their curricula. Recently, some basal reading series have upgraded their textbooks with literary selections. At the end of selections, readings are sometimes suggested that extend a story through related stories and books. The whole language approach, an alternative to basal readers, integrates all communication and language skills in lessons where children read, write, and discuss their reactions to language. Many teachers employ popular, current, and well-known children's literature in class as reading texts.

Teachers whose goal is to produce lifelong readers and literate learners must be ready to use a wide variety of materials and to seek successful ideas and techniques. This book helps teachers and media directors to enrich elementary reading programs with children's literature and to pursue sound educational objectives as they share the books and stories.

Glenna Sloan identifies a literate person as "not one who knows how to read, but one who reads fluently, responsively, critically, and because he (or she) wants to."[1] Every teacher of elementary reading hopes to give children the power and the desire to read. There are many ways to empower children. Two current methods will be discussed briefly, as will reasons to enrich each with literature. Teachers who wish to read a full discussion on reading methods and theories should consult professional books on reading.

Many children are currently taught to read using a basal reading series. Each series has a research-based definition of reading and a scope and sequence of the consistent skills. Word lists are generated for different levels, and stories are written with these words. These series are available with workbooks and tests for assessing levels and skills. Basal reading series are valuable tools for teaching the skills of word recognition and phonics and for giving practice in functional vocabulary. Because of their controlled vocabulary and short thought units, however, they lead some children (and teachers) to think that reading is saying the right words in the right places on the page.

Children need the skills provided by basal readers, but they need *more* experiences during the critical first years of education. Basal readers alone cannot provide enough experiences for all children learning to read their language. Controlled vocabularies and contents can limit imagination and motivation of learners.

Educators who use basal readers are challenged to give students varied experiences with stories outside the textbook. Teachers can use their basal series, enrich the curriculum with reading strategies and literature from this book, and enhance their contributions to creating literate students—children who can read and choose to do so.

Recently, educators have been teaching reading by integrating reading with writing and with all language study. This *whole language approach* concentrates children's efforts on expressing and gaining meaning. Writing, reading, spelling, and punctuation are all seen as means toward successful communication. This approach calls for meaningful experiences with relevant stories and books. Children are expected to write and communicate in functional ways that arise from genuine language needs. Often, children read and write for sustained lengths of time to improve the flexibility and fluency of their receptive and expressive language skills. Children are shown that all communication must be meaningful.

Teachers using the whole language approach often do not use specific texts or they adapt textbooks for their own purpose. They constantly need materials that are interesting and appropriate for children. They also need activities that are consistent with the integrated use of language. This book will serve as a resource for teachers using the whole language method of reading instruction. Both the literary works and the activities fit many learning situations designed to foster successful learning.

Besides being suitable for major approaches to teaching reading, the use of literature in the reading program is important for other reasons: to promote a love of reading and allow students emotional connections with the characters and ideas in literature, to encourage deeper understanding and higher level thinking, and to use materials that hold significance for young readers.

Charlotte Huck outlines the value of literature for children and lists the ways literature can expand children's worlds:

1. Literature can help children develop insights and understandings of the world.
2. Literature can help children develop imagination.
3. Literature helps children develop their "interior landscape," to visualize settings and events.
4. Literature helps children develop a sense of wonder and joy in living.[2]

Literature enriches the lives and education of children. It can be used in the classroom to show students that people are alike in many ways, that many others have had similar experiences and feelings. Children need to know that they are not alone when they feel lonely, angry, deserted. Children can test their ideas against the ideas they find in books. Children can make startling new discoveries in literature; they can experience danger and adventure while sitting safely at school. Children need experiences with books in order to find themselves within books and to gain new perspectives.

Authors and illustrators of children's books communicate so vividly that the reader, miles and perhaps years away, can share the emotions, experiences, and ideas depicted. The reader must bring all his or her skills and knowledge to reading to share in full the author's message. The reader's motivation for this task is enjoyment. With the concepts and classroom activities presented in *this* book, teachers can encourage children to "connect" with literature. When teachers share their own enjoyment and love of literature with their students, the children understand that there is great joy inherent in literature. Kenneth Goodman, reading educator and pioneer in psycholinguistics, sees the need to include literary materials "because of their aesthetic, stylistic qualities" in any program teaching reading. They "yield a kind of pleasure and satisfaction which creates further appetite for literature."[3]

Trying to instill a love of learning with any one approach to reading is very difficult. Often, because of the simpler content of stories, comprehension objectives tend to fall in the lower levels of Bloom's taxonomy of cognitive learning. Children are asked to recall, name, repeat, memorize, restate, and locate. These are vital skills, but children are capable of more. The learning taxonomy defined by Benjamin Bloom[4] identifies different levels of performance and experiences within educational tasks. As students move beyond recall and translation of knowledge to analyzing, applying, and evaluating knowledge, their depth of understanding increases. Bloom avoids value judgments about one level of objectives over another, but as students manipulate information at higher levels, they are on their way to becoming independent, self-confident readers and learners. Predicting and identifying patterns and sequences in literature, and using visual clues to enrich the meaning, are consistent with Bloom's model.

Identifying the literary elements of plot and characterization or noting the nuances introduced through figurative language are thinking skills within the intellectual reach of young readers. These skills, as well as selecting, correcting, inferring, comparing, contrasting, and interpreting are the higher level thinking skills necessary to successful reading. The activities in this book have been selected so that higher levels of thinking are expected and encouraged.

Another educational need met by including literature in the reading program is motivation through relevant, significant material.

Literature is created to express meaning and children naturally expect to understand. Teachers must build lessons on this fact. Don Holdaway, a New Zealand educator, feels that teachers need to ensure success in learning by making the materials for learning relevant and interesting. He calls for "a program based on the immediate utility of real life language, enriched by copious experience of memorable story, poem, and song."[5] With teachers choosing the books and stories and guiding student experiences, relevancy can be assured. Goodman argues: "It's hard to motivate kids when the stuff they are asked to read, write, hear and say has no relation to who they are, what they think, and what they do."[6]

WHO CAN USE THIS BOOK?

Any educator who is committed to providing the best reading program for beginning and young readers will benefit from this book. No matter what instructional method is used, the activities in this book will expand and enrich the opportunities for children to become literate. Charlotte Huck recommends to all teachers that "instead of going back to the basics and giving children more and more skills, we should free children to discover the pleasures of reading."[7]

Teachers who now use a basal series exclusively can use the objectives included in the work to give children extra opportunities to hear and read quality literature, to encourage children to respond in depth to ideas and emotions in literature, and to give time for the practice of predicting, sequencing, and recognizing literary patterns. Kenneth Goodman advises: "Read to and with children individually and in small groups. Encourage them to follow, predict, read along and even take over if they choose."[8] The literary selections suggested here will enable teachers to give more such opportunities to children. This book is a tool to allow teachers to address the need for children to read widely in order to practice their literacy and begin to form ideas and judgments.

Teachers who are combining a basal program and a modified whole language program can easily use the reading-listening-discussing-writing activities as a natural, intentional part of the reading curriculum. The combination of skills instruction in the basal series, experiences with literature, and the chance to discuss, write, or respond through discussion, role-playing, and art will enrich the offerings to students.

Many teachers who are using a whole language program will be familiar with a number of the ideas and books offered here. For those teachers, this book can serve as a reference to enhance their repertoire of ideas and activities. All the activities are designed to build the comprehension aptitudes of children.

Library media specialists will find in this book a positive contribution to the reading curriculum of their schools. Using media center visits planned with the teacher, the specialist can introduce concepts and activities, modeling a creative teaching style that motivates children. The specialist will want to share these activities with teachers who are open to innovations and are committed to introducing literature to their students.

HOW CAN THIS BOOK BE USED?

The book has been arranged by levels: kindergarten, transitional, and first grade activities; second and third grade activities; and fourth and fifth grade activities. Each level presents units with objectives appropriate to the students' abilities. Each unit opens with student objectives and an annotated bibliography. This "Recommended Reading" list gives the numbers of the student objectives that the book illustrates. Activities for each of the books follow the bibliography. All suggested books have been reviewed favorably in retrospective or current selection tools, and all are deemed appropriate for the grade level indicated.

Each unit is introduced by a detailed group activity. Teacher directions for each level are written in language appropriate to the age of the students (so that the teacher can easily use them to direct the students), and a difference is apparent between the levels. The group activities are organized in the same manner throughout the book. Instructions for teacher preparation list books to obtain and any materials that will be needed. Suggestions for focusing students' attention reflect the vocabulary of children at different reading levels. The objective for each group activity is stated. The description of the group activity is detailed, with specific questions suggested as well as ways to guide the students' thinking. These suggestions should not limit relevant student responses or discussion. An extending activity follows as a way to bring closure and to provide an opportunity for the students to respond to the literature. Often there is a product that the students create and share with the class. Creating, sharing, and listening to the observations of others are powerful learning tools and will result in a growing appreciation of reading and of literature.

Following the introductory activity for each unit are additional activities for the other books. The teachers may choose to include as many of the activities as they deem appropriate for the students. All these activities are suggestions—creative, innovative teaching is encouraged. The techniques and ideas listed will easily lend themselves to other books and literary works.

Extending activities for the books give the students an opportunity to reflect on the story they have shared, and to encourage them to interpret the story with visual arts, creative dramatics, or writing. Teachers are encouraged to have their students write class books and to display students' artwork and writings on bulletin boards or murals for all to see. This validates the efforts of the students and shows them that they, too, are authors and illustrators. Students will realize that communication and comprehension are valuable tools for all people, and that they are capable of both. They will understand that writing, drawing, and reading are all creative activities.

Some of the extending activities are class discussions. It is vitally important that young students have the opportunity to express their interpretations of and feelings about literature and listen to those who may feel differently. During these discussions, the teacher should allow time to develop an atmosphere of trust and acceptance so that even the quiet, observing students, those who hesitate to risk an idea, will be encouraged to share. Students should feel accepted by their teacher and their classmates during these discussions, know that their opinions and ideas are important views to be respected, and recognize that they are capable of interpreting literature and sharing their individual views. These discussions should include many open-ended questions that lead students to share their personal responses: what they like or didn't like, how the work made them feel, what was important to remember, how the ideas connect with other information. Students should be asked to identify with characters, to compare and contrast action, and to assess motives in relation to their own.

The units and objectives are presented in a sequential manner so that teachers can continue the work begun by instructors at lower grades. If teachers are introducing the concepts in this book, they may wish to sample the activities of the lower grades for additional ideas. Because every classroom is different, teachers should adapt units and activities to fit the needs and abilities of their students.

The units are very stable between the kindergarten/transitional/ first grade level (K–T–1) and the second grade/third grade level (2–3); the same wide-reaching goals are in place. For the fourth grade/fifth grade level (4–5), there is a restructuring of the units to allow for integrated study of literary genres using a literary analysis approach to literature. Literary terms introduced to the students are listed in the glossary at the end of the book. Using the literary terms is extremely important, for internalization of the concepts comes after repeated exposures. For a more detailed discussion of genres and literary terms, teachers may find it useful to consult Rebecca Lukens' *A Critical Handbook of Children's Literature,* a work that makes literary criticism accessible to children.[9]

Kindergarten/transitional/first grade activities are planned for children who have little or no word recognition skills. Activities are led by the teacher, with the reading being done by the teacher. Children are encouraged to predict, recognize language patterns, and often to join the teacher at appropriate times during reading. Children are introduced to simple ideas of characterization and plot line. Visual literacy is stressed as a way to gain a deeper understanding of the story. Figurative language is examined, and examples are collected. During all discussions, students should be encouraged to take an active part in responding to the stories and ideas. Teachers may choose to continue some discussions well beyond the suggested questions.

The activities for grades 2 and 3 include some individual activities that can be completed by independent readers. This level still has many books that are read by the teacher and discussed by the class. This allows less able readers to hear and see successful models of comprehension. The same strands that were introduced in the K–T–1 level are continued in 2–3, with more literary terms defined and used. Information books are included as a transition to the genre study of the next level.

There is a reorganization of the units for the grade levels 4 and 5. All literary terms are used within the discussions of specific literature genres. Poetry, contemporary fiction, modern fantasy, biography, as well as classics of children's literature are forms that are pursued. Teachers serve as facilitators because the activities are designed for the students to complete independently. Students discuss the merits of literary works and participate in literary criticism. Visual literacy is continued as a separate strand and activities are of corresponding sophistication.

At this level it may not be possible for teachers to have read all the suggested books. This need not create a problem, because teachers can judge the quality of the student activity without being familiar with the book. Teachers should feel free to ask the students questions about their books to learn more. Because reading abilities vary from above level to below level in any classroom, selections have been included to allow teachers to lead students to appropriate books.

In November 1988 the National Council of Teachers of English passed a resolution that included a call for a critical assessment of basal reading programs and their underlying premises. This resolution addressed the need to:

1. Support teachers . . . developing programs fostering literacy
2. Encourage administrators to allow alternatives (and) . . . enable teachers to determine materials and means that foster literacy
3. Encourage and support . . . a broad, functional and learner centered concept of literacy[10]

The NCTE recommended that teachers develop innovative strategies to teach reading, and that teachers work to understand the relationship of reading to learning and to writing. The ideas that follow in this book stride toward strengthening and broadening teachers' use of materials and strategies in enriching the education of young children. If teachers will use the concepts, ideas, and activities in this book in their classrooms, they will be making a contribution toward helping children become truly literate—able and eager to read.

REFERENCES

1. Glenna Sloan, *The Child as Critic* (New York: Columbia Teachers College Press, 1984), p. 1.

2. Charlotte Huck, "I Give You the End of a Golden String," *Theory Into Practice* (21, no. 4): p. 317.

3. Kenneth Goodman, *Reading: Process and Program* (Urbana, IL: National Council of Teachers of English, 1975), p. 20.

4. Benjamin Bloom, ed., *The Taxonomy of Education Objectives. Handbook I. Cognitive Domain* (New York: Longmans, Green, 1956).

5. Don Holdaway, *Stability and Change in Literacy Learning* (Exeter, NH: Heinemann Educational Books, 1984), p. 25.

6. Kenneth Goodman, *What's Whole in Whole Language?* (Portsmouth, NH: Heinemann, 1986), p. 9.

7. Huck, "End of a Golden String," p. 318.

8. Goodman, *Whole Language,* p. 45.

9. Rebecca Lukens, *A Critical Handbook of Children's Literature,* 4th ed. (Glenview, IL: Scott, Foresman, 1990).

10. "Point/Counterpoint: The Value of Basal Readers," *Reading Today* (August/September 1989): p. 1.

LITERATURE-BASED READING

Children's Books and Activities to Enrich the K-5 Curriculum

Chapter 1
Kindergarten/Transitional/
First Grade

The activities in this chapter are designed for the child who is beginning to make sense of print but may not be reading. The skills and strategies these activities strengthen have been identified by reading experts as vital for the young child. Prediction and recognizing patterned stories build on the natural language strengths that each child possesses. Children expect language, including written language, to make sense, and prediction and patterns reinforce that expectation. Children can sequence events in their lives in an unorganized, natural way. The teacher must elicit discussion of sequence in stories. Young children are capable of identifying with people and empathizing with their problems. Beginning to discuss these concepts at this level makes children aware of the importance of character and plot in fiction. One of the main objectives of any beginning reading program is to introduce children to the written word, to enlarge their reading vocabulary. Children are also capable of responding to the imagery of figurative language and, with the teacher's help, of comprehending the deeper meanings of the images. Visual literacy is extremely important to young children. Children respond strongly to pictures and look for clues to meaning within illustrations. The teacher can build on this natural tendency and train children to be careful observers and interpreters.

Although activities are shared in a large group, communication and creativity are expected of each child. Time for discussion and follow-up are included to give children ample opportunities to learn from one another and to practice listening and speaking. Often a creative activity will follow the group activity to help the children interact with words and ideas of the stories after the initial reading. Teachers who merely read a story to children, close the book, and go on to another activity or curricular area are missing a crucial opportunity to help children internalize the work and make it theirs. Writing or dictating to an older writer is another important activity for this level, because material written by children is highly motivating, both for the young author and for classmates, who will be his or her readers.

Visual Literacy

STUDENT OBJECTIVES:

1. Tell a story using pictures only.
2. Find details or hidden objects in illustrations that enhance the story read.
3. Identify a whole from a part.
4. Identify words from pictures.

RECOMMENDED READING:

Briggs, Raymond. *The Snowman.* Random House, 1978, 1986. (Objective 1)
   In a wordless picture book a little boy builds a snowman that visits his house and takes a flight with the boy over the world.
Carle, Eric. *Do You Want to Be My Friend?* Thomas Y. Crowell, 1971. (Objectives 1, 3)
   Children must identify each animal after seeing only the tail in this wordless picture book of a mouse seeking a friend.
Euvremer, Teryl. *Sun's Up.* Crown, 1987. (Objective 1)
   The personified sun carries on his day's activities in this wordless picture book.
Hoban, Lillian. *Look! Look! Look!* Greenwillow, 1988. (Objective 3)
   Photographs of dogs, an elephant's tail, etc. are viewed first through a cut-out square, then in entirety.
Hutchins, Pat. *Changes, Changes.* Macmillan, 1971. (Objectives 1, 3)
   In a wordless picture book a wooden man and woman change the configuration of blocks to solve their problems.
Jonas, Ann. *The Trek.* Greenwillow, 1985. (Objective 2)
   Close observation of visual clues aids in the identification of the many imaginary animals encountered on the way to school.
McMillan, Bruce. *Dry or Wet?* Lothrop, Lee & Shepard, 1988. (Objective 4)
   Paired photographs of scenes depict dryness and wetness.

Mother Goose. *The Real Mother Goose Picture Word Rhymes.* Illustrated by Blanche Fisher Wright. Macmillan, 1987. (Objective 4)
Rebus format is used to present familiar rhymes.

Parnall, Peter. *Feet!* Macmillan, 1988. (Objectives 3, 4)
Pen and ink watercolor illustrations introduce all kinds of animal feet from webbed to dirty.

Rees, Mary. *Ten in a Bed.* Little, Brown, 1988. (Objectives 1, 2)
Illustrations depict a humorous story to accompany the familiar rhyme.

Sewall, Marcia. *Animal Song.* Little, Brown, 1988. (Objective 1)
The name of the animals is the only text provided to assist children in telling the picture story of the animals' preparations for crow's party.

Spier, Peter. *Dreams.* Doubleday, 1986. (Objective 1)
Fantasy scenes appear to the children as they view the changing clouds.

Tafuri, Nancy. *Do Not Disturb.* Greenwillow, 1987. (Objective 1)
Almost wordless story of a family's camping activities that scared the animals.

Tafuri, Nancy. *Junglewalk.* Greenwillow, 1988. (Objectives 1, 2)
A wordless picture book of a little boy who dreams of seeing wild animals after reading a book about jungles.

Tafuri, Nancy. *Spots, Feathers and Curly Tails.* Greenwillow, 1988. (Objective 3)
Questions and illustrations of parts of the animal's body are used to highlight physical characteristics of various animals.

GROUP INTRODUCTORY ACTIVITY:

Preparing for the Activity: Locate Lillian Hoban's *Look! Look! Look!* Be certain that you have a large selection of pictures from magazines, glue, paper on which to glue the photos, and paper to use as cover masks for the pictures. Cut a three-inch square in a poster board.

Focus: Show the children a large, colorful picture of a clearly identifiable object. Discuss the object and its various properties. Now take the poster board from which you have cut a three-inch square. Place the poster board mask over the picture and discuss what clues are visible to identify the whole picture. Move the mask to expose different visual details. Ask, each time you move the mask, what clues can be used to identify the picture.

Objective: To satisfy the objective of identifying a whole after seeing a part, introduce Lillian Hoban's *Look! Look! Look!* Tell the class that this book will show a small detail of a bigger object, and their job is to tell what the whole object is.

Guided Activity: As you show the first picture of a portion of a collie dog, have the children think out loud and listen to each other. Have the group make several logical guesses. Then turn the page and expose the collie and leash. When you turn to the next page, the children see the picture of the same collie and leash, this time connected to a person. Then display the next page and repeat the process of listening and guessing.

After revealing the ball of yarn, ask who (or what) could be using the yarn. What could the elephant be doing? Who is enjoying the rose? What is connected to the wrinkled foot? Whose guitar is that? What do we use pumpkins for? Reinforce with positive remarks whenever children use words that show their careful observation.

Extending Activity: Let the children make a book similar to Hoban's. Have magazines and white paper available. Let the children tear a photograph from the magazines and paste it on white paper. Give each child another piece of white paper for a mask. Suggest that each child cut a hole in the white paper in the best place for someone else to guess the object. Then match each mask with the picture and assemble for a small book. Suggest that the children look at Hoban's book from back to front. This examination goes from a large view to a close-up.

FOLLOW-UP ACTIVITIES FOR TEACHER AND STUDENTS TO SHARE:

1. Share Raymond Briggs' *The Snowman* with the children. As they carefully examine each page, let them name the boy and tell the story. Be sure the children notice and comment on each activity or object shared by the boy and the snowman when they tour the boy's house. After they have "read" the story, divide the children into pairs. Have each pair name a familiar object that the snowman saw in the house and asked about. After discussion with the teacher or media specialist and after a bit of practice, have the pairs of children act out the boy's explanation of the use of each object and the snowman's reaction.
2. Before showing Eric Carle's *Do You Want to Be My Friend?* to the class, explain that the book is wordless so the children will need to help read it. Let children tell you what animal the mouse is talking to as they view each tail. Then let the children decide what each animal says or does to drive the mouse away when he seeks friendship. Let the children predict why the two mice hide in the hole in the tree instead of following the green path farther.

    Explain to the children that Carle used collage for the illustrations and did not use any color for the background. Does this make it easier for them to follow the story? Let the children tear brown paper and glue the pieces onto white paper to make a mouse portrait.

3. As you show Teryl Euvremer's *Sun's Up* to the children, let them locate the sun on each page and identify its activities as the day progresses. Talk about the activities that children also do. After completing the story, let the children suppose the main character was the moon. What night activities could he engage in? Ask the children each to illustrate a favorite idea to make a class book "The Moon's Up." Encourage them to use their imagination.

4. Turn the pages of *Changes, Changes* by Pat Hutchins for the children, letting them name the characters and tell the story as they read the pictures. Be sure to have them identify each crisis that causes the two characters to make changes in the object they built. The children may want to predict what the characters will build before seeing each finished product. At the end of the story have the children contrast the final house with that built at the beginning. What is missing? Why is there no arch on the second house? Give pairs of children some building blocks so they can build and change their construction as they identify a problem that makes a change necessary.

5. Read aloud Ann Jonas's *The Trek*. Let the children identify the imaginary animal dangers that are lurking. Have the children identify each of the animals pictured at the end. How many did they name as they studied the pictures? Re-examine the pictures to see if all animals can be found. With the help of older students or parent volunteers, take the children in small groups on a neighborhood walk. Let the leader record the pretend animals the children saw and the actual object that sparked their imagination.

6. As you display each pair of pages in Bruce McMillan's *Dry or Wet?*, ask the children to point to the page that shows the idea of *wet* and the page that shows the idea of *dry*. Ask them what clue they used to make each decision. Call attention to the fact that the artist chose photographs as the medium for presenting the concepts. Discuss the advantage of using photographs for this book.

   Have the children think of other opposite pairs such as hot or cold. Let them use old magazines to locate pictures to illustrate those concepts. Label each pair and display them on a bulletin board labeled *Opposites*.

7. Before beginning each rebus rhyme in *The Real Mother Goose Picture Word Rhymes* with the students, have them identify the words at the bottom of the page so they can participate in reading the rhyme. Have children think of other nursery rhymes and pictures that could be used to make a rebus of the rhyme. Let older children or adult volunteers work with small groups of

children to create a rebus nursery rhyme, using the children's suggestions.

8. Read Peter Parnall's *Feet!* with the class. Beginning with the title page have the children examine the illustration of an animal foot and locate the small picture of the animal that will help in identification. Share the brief text and illustrations on each double-spread page and let the children identify the animal illustrated in the picture. Then go back through the text and have the children think of other animals that could have been used for fast feet, slow feet, etc. Cut out feet from an animal coloring book. See if the children can identify each animal.

9. Read Mary Rees's *Ten in a Bed,* urging the children to join in as you repeat the lines until none are left in bed. If you know the melody, have the children sing the song. Now go back through the book again and let the children tell the humorous illustrated story of the children's escapades as they continue to fall out of bed.

10. Introduce Marcia Sewall's *Animal Song* by showing the children the animals' pictures on the end pages of the book. Let them identify each animal. Now share the story, letting the children examine each picture in order to invent the story of the party preparations and the festivities that ensued. After the children complete the story, teach them the simple tune and let them sing it. Use the end paper illustrations to prompt their memories of the alphabetical sequence of events.

11. Look at Peter Spier's *Dreams* with the class. As children examine the double-spread illustrations of the clouds, let them reconstruct verbally the fantasy scenes the children are dreaming. After they have enjoyed Spier's book, take the children outside on a day when the sky is filled with fluffy clouds and urge them to imagine scenes from the shapes. When the class returns to the room, ask them to recall ideas, words, and scenes that they imagined. Write their contributions on the board. Let each child pick a favorite idea and illustrate it, using light blue paper, chalk, and pencil. A quick squirt of hair spray will "fix" the chalk. Copy their words on each picture and display.

12. Show the pictures in Nancy Tafuri's *Do Not Disturb* and let the children tell the story. After completing the book, let the children recall the animals that were disturbed. Think of others that could have been seen. How might the family have disturbed each of those named? What noise could those animals have made at night to disturb the family's sleep? Let each child pick an animal and join in an animal chorus.

13. Before presenting Nancy Tafuri's *Junglewalk,* ask the children to suggest animals they might see in the jungle. Then let them study each textless page to decipher the story of the boy's dream. Give them time to describe each animal's actions. Find the boy's picture in order to discuss his reaction. After complet-

ing the story, check to see if the children saw all of the animals
listed on the dustjacket. With them, go through the book again
to locate any animals missed in the first telling.

Compare the animals the boy saw with the ones the children suggested before looking at the story. What new animals
did they learn? Referring to the dustjacket, tell the children the
continent each animal lived in. With them, locate the continents
on the globe. Count the continents involved in the boy's dream.
14. Read Nancy Tafuri's *Spots, Feathers and Curly Tails* to the
class. Do not show the picture until the children answer each
question. When the book is finished, let the children think of
unique characteristics of other animals, such as scales and
stripes.

Predicting

STUDENT OBJECTIVES:

1. Forecast the next word in a story or poem being read.
2. Predict the ending of a story.
3. Predict "what happens next" in a story.
4. Justify a prediction with details from the story to use as docu-
mentation.

RECOMMENDED READING:

Brown, Marc. *Play Rhymes.* E. P. Dutton, 1987. (Objective 1)
Twelve familiar rhymes are illustrated with actions; six also have
music.
Brown, Margaret Wise. *The Runaway Bunny.* Illustrated by Clement
Hurd. Harper & Row, 1942, 1972. (Objectives 2, 3, 4)
Each time the little bunny says he will run away, his loving
mother suggests an appropriate way to find him.
Ekker, Ernst A. *What Is Beyond the Hill?* Illustrated by Hilde
Heyduck-Huth. J. B. Lippincott, 1986. (Objective 3)
The children take an imaginary journey over the next hill and
finally to the stars.

Goodall, John S. *Shrewbettina's Birthday.* Harcourt Brace Jovanovich, 1970, op., 1983, paper. (Objective 3)
A dainty mouse has an adventure-filled day in this wordless picture book that invites prediction.

Hague, Kathleen. *Alphabears.* Illustrated by Michael Hague. Henry Holt, 1984. (Objective 1)
Each bear is named in alphabetical order and a characteristic is given in a rhyming text.

Hutchins, Pat. *Where's the Baby?* Greenwillow, 1988. (Objectives 2, 3)
Sister, mother, and grandmother do not know where Baby Monster is, but they only have to see the mess to know where he has been.

Lloyd, David. *Hello, Goodbye.* Illustrated by Louise Voce. Lothrop, Lee & Shepard, 1988. (Objective 3)
Creatures meet at a tree and say hello. Then the rain forces them to say goodbye.

Mother Goose. *If Wishes Were Horses.* Illustrated by Susan Jeffers. E. P. Dutton, 1979. (Objective 1)
Combines several nursery rhymes about horses to create a new delight for readers.

Petersham, Maud and Miska. *The Box with Red Wheels.* Macmillan, 1949. (Objectives 2, 3, 4)
The animals try to guess what is in the box, and the result is a pleasant surprise.

Potter, Beatrix. *The Tale of Benjamin Bunny.* Frederick Warne, 1903. (Objectives 2, 3, 4)
Peter Rabbit and his cousin, Benjamin Bunny, return to Mr. McGregor's garden to retrieve Peter's coat and shoes.

Titherington, Jeanne. *A Place for Ben.* Greenwillow, 1987. (Objectives 2, 3, 4)
Although Ben resents his baby brother's being in his room, he becomes lonely when he finds a place of his own.

Winthrop, Elizabeth. *Shoes.* Illustrated by William Joyce. Harper & Row, 1986. (Objective 1)
Simple rhyming text identifies many kinds of and uses for shoes, but shows going barefoot is best.

Wood, Audrey. *King Bidgood's in the Bathtub.* Illustrated by Don Wood. Harcourt Brace Jovanovich, 1985. (Objectives 2, 3)
After members of the court fail in their ideas of how to get the fun-loving king out of the bathtub, the page solves the problem.

Zolotow, Charlotte. *But Not Billy.* Illustrated by Kay Chorao. Harper & Row, 1985. (Objectives 1, 4)
Billy's mother ceases giving him loving nicknames when he calls her Mama.

GROUP INTRODUCTORY ACTIVITY:

Preparing for the Activity: Locate Beatrix Potter's *The Tale of Benjamin Bunny.*

Focus: Direct the children to look at the chalkboard. Tell them that you will draw a picture on the board, step by step. Tell them that their job is to guess what the picture might be from the clues they see. Draw the first line of the picture on the board and ask volunteers to guess. (See the end of the "Group Introductory Activity" section for steps in drawing.) Choose self-confident children who won't be upset if they've guessed wrong. Tell the class that guessing can be a worthwhile risk and that making a wrong guess is all right. Write the guesses on the board beside the picture. Read each word as you write it. Take only five volunteers each time.

Add another detail. Review the first guesses, and evaluate each with the new detail. Does each guess seem logical with the new information? Cross off any words that don't fit the second detail. Ask for new guesses now. Read as you write on the board. Continue this pattern of detail, review, guess. Try to include everyone in the activity. As you guide this activity, use the words *guess, logical,* and *risk.*

By the time the cat is revealed you will probably have the word *cat* on the board. Circle that word, erase the others, and ask the class to tell you what they found out about guessing.

Objective: To satisfy the objective of predicting what will happen next, predicting the ending of the entry, and justifying predictions, tell the children that thoughtful guessing is an important part of reading stories. They must always be listening and ready to guess what could happen next. Say that they will have practice in thoughtful guessing, or in predicting what will happen next in this story.

Guided Activity: Introduce Beatrix Potter's *The Tale of Benjamin Bunny,* saying that this adventure follows Peter Rabbit's first trip into Mr. McGregor's garden. Have the children recall *The Tale of Peter Rabbit.* Tell the class that a cat will play an important part in this story. Ask for predictions of what a cat could have to do with a bunny. Explain that this story happens right after Peter Rabbit escapes from Mr. McGregor's garden, and that Peter and Benjamin are cousins. Ask if anyone has a prediction about what might happen.

Read the story. Stop when Peter and Benjamin are looking down at the garden and ask for predictions. Praise logical predictions, telling the children that those predictions make sense in the story. Model how to return to earlier details to support a prediction. Say, "Let's see if the author thought of any of our ideas." Read on. If predictions were not correct, tell the class that the author had another idea for the story, and that their predictions are still very good if they make sense. Remind the children that they can find clues for their predictions in the words and pictures.

Stop at the first view of the cat. Ask for predictions again. One way to involve the timid children who are afraid to predict and be wrong is to ask everyone to signal "thumbs up" when they have made a prediction, even though you will not ask them to respond. This allows all children to feel a part of the activity, and more important, to gain confidence about offering their predictions. Emphasize that although guessing means taking a risk, all predictions that make sense are good guesses. Read on. Stop for predictions on the final outcome, when Mr. Benjamin Bunny appears. Finish the book.

Extending Activity: Ask the children to predict another adventure for Benjamin and Peter. Will they go back to Mr. McGregor's garden? Why or why not? Have the class draw a picture of what Peter and Benjamin might do next. Bring the group together to share their pictures and ideas. Close by telling the children to predict three more times during the day—the lunch menu, which bus comes first, and the first thing an adult will say to them when they arrive home. The important thing is that children use the word *predict*, and that they intentionally predict.

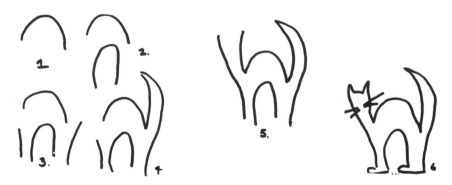

FOLLOW-UP ACTIVITIES FOR TEACHER AND STUDENTS TO SHARE:

1. Read "Animals" from Marc Brown's *Play Rhymes* to the class. Search the illustrations with the students to find clues as they predict the end of each line of the rhyme—for example, "hop like a _____ ." Reread, having the class act out the lines as they participate in saying them.

   Now read "Wheel on the Bus" to the class. Have the children predict what the driver, children, and mothers will say before completing the line. Let the children repeat the lines that complete each verse. Read the poem again, this time having the children say the lines and do the finger play. They may want to sing the lines. Use the music given at the back of the book. Read the other poems in a similar manner at another time.

2. Read to the class *The Runaway Bunny* by Margaret Wise Brown. Stop reading each time the little bunny suggests how he will run away, and let the children predict how the mother will catch him. Let the children tell how they were able to make the prediction. Just before the end of the story, let the children predict how it will end.

   After completing the story, tell the children the story was written in 1942 when their grandmothers were young. What different ways could the baby rabbit suggest he would run away today? For each of their suggestions how might the mother catch him?

3. Introduce Ernst Ekker's *What Is Beyond the Hill?* by asking the children to suggest things they see as they go up over a hill while riding in a car. Read the book to the class. Stop after each question so the children can predict what is beyond the object they are seeing. As a follow-up do a "remembering/sequencing" activity with the class as they develop the simple text for a "What Is Beyond Our Classroom Door" story patterned after Ekker's book.

4. Explain the unique format of John Goodall's *Shrewbettina's Birthday* in which a half-page will cover the author's answer to the children's prediction. Share each two-page spread and have the children raise their hands or put "thumbs up" when they have a logical guess. Ask two children to share their predictions aloud. Then say "Let's see what the author thought," and turn the half-page. Always reward logical thinking with comments such as "That was a good idea that Mr. Goodall could have used." After completing the book, discuss the half-page format. Why do they suppose it was used for this book?

5. Read Kathleen Hague's *Alphabears* aloud to the class. Let the children try to fill in the last word on each page before reading it. Reread the rhymes and let children identify the ones that use other words within the rhymes beginning with the same letter as the names. Invite children to bring stuffed bears for a library or classroom display. After the child tells the name of the bear, let the children participate in making an appropriate two-line rhyme. Record the rhymes on a card to accompany each bear displayed.

6. Introduce Pat Hutchins' *Where's the Baby?* to the class by telling them the book has picture clues they can use to predict the answer to the title. Read the first page and point out the baby hiding behind the door. When Hazel follows the footprints to the kitchen, ask for predictions about the kind of mess a baby could make in a kitchen. Then turn the page to see, and find the baby again. Continue looking at the clues from room to room,

letting the children predict the mess before turning the page. Let the children predict what kind of comment Grandma will make. When everyone leaves the sleeping baby's room, have the class predict the ending.

As a follow-up let the children make a portrait of Hazel or the baby, using chocolate pudding as their medium on heavy art paper. Use instant pudding with the consistency of commercial finger paints. Have each child clean up the mess as baby did not.

7. Read David Lloyd's *Hello, Goodbye* to the class. After the big red bird says "Hello," have the children guess who could be in the tree to answer. After squeaky voices on branches say "Hello," ask for predictions about another part of the tree where animals could be. Have the students continue predicting as you read text.

   If the story had been about a cat near a rosebush, what animals or insects might have answered him? Using the pattern of *Hello, Goodbye,* let children make up the cat story and play it out with the teacher or librarian adding needed narration.

8. Tell the children that you will read each rhyme twice in Mother Goose's *If Wishes Were Horses,* illustrated by Susan Jeffers. The first time you won't show the pictures so they can listen. As you read it again, they will be able to see the pictures and join in as they wish. Read the first rhyme, stopping before the last word in the last line. Remind the children the omitted word will rhyme with "ride." Read the rhymes, pausing to let the children try to fill in the rhyming word. When you finish the book, read it aloud again and show the illustrations. Pause each time to let the children fill in the rhyming words. Let children act out their favorite rhyme.

9. Introduce Maud and Miska Petersham's *The Box with Red Wheels* by telling the children they will need to listen carefully and observe the pictures closely in order to predict. After reading the first page, ask the children to predict what is in the box. Write their ideas on the board. Continue reading. As each new character is introduced, ask for predictions of what is in the box. As the story progresses, cross out any ideas on the blackboard that the children no longer think are valid. Add new ones. When the baby is revealed, check the board to see if that was anyone's original prediction. When the baby is sad, ask what the mother will do to make everyone happy. Complete the book. Reread to collect the clues that helped children predict. Why did the house pets know what the farm animals did not? As a follow-up ask the children to think of other animals and guess how they would react to the box.

10. Before reading Jeanne Titherington's *A Place for Ben,* ask the children if they ever want a place where they can be alone. If so, what can they do to make such a special place? (For example,

they could cover a card table with a sheet and crawl under it.) Read the story to the children. Stop after the line "Finally he found the perfect place" and see if the class can predict where it is. Continue the story. After reading the sentence "Everything was ready but still something wasn't right," have the children predict what was wrong. Read on until Ben sits on the step waiting for a visitor. Have the children predict the ending and document why they made each suggestion. Complete the story. Let the children suggest a list of things Ben could play with his little brother that both would enjoy.

11. Read Elizabeth Winthrop's *Shoes* aloud to the class, stopping to let the children predict each rhyming word before reading it. As a follow-up have some pictures of coats from a catalog to share with the children. Let them make a "use" verse for the different coats.

12. Before sharing Audrey Wood's *King Bidgood's in the Bathtub,* divide the group in half. Suggest that whenever you point to one group, they will cry, "Help, help!" When you point to the other group they will say, "Oh, who knows what to do?" Let them practice the lines twice so they can create an appropriate feeling of desperation. Read the story with the groups' participation. Stop after the court cries "Help, help!" Let the children predict what will happen. Then continue to see how the page solved the problem.

13. Before reading Charlotte Zolotow's *But Not Billy* to the class, let the children think of loving terms parents sometimes call babies. Read the story to the class without sharing the illustrations. As soon as you read the sound the baby makes or a description of the baby's appearance, stop reading before the animal is named. Let the children predict what the mother will call the baby. Then encourage them to participate in the repetition "But not Billy." Complete the story, letting them predict each animal. Have the children retell the story from the pictures. Discuss how they were able to predict each animal. See if the children can think of other animals and a situation or sound that would make the mother give the baby that name.

Patterns in Literature

STUDENT OBJECTIVES:

1. Find repeating words and phrases in stories.
2. Identify progressive events in a patterned story after hearing it read.
3. Anticipate phrases that accompany additional characters or actions in a cumulative story.
4. Write a new book as a parody of simply patterned texts in picture books.

RECOMMENDED READING:

Brown, Margaret Wise. *Wait Till the Moon Is Full.* Illustrated by Garth Williams. Harper & Row, 1948. (Objectives 1, 3)
The little raccoon impatiently waits for a full moon so he can go out into the woods and see the night.

Carle, Eric. *The Very Busy Spider.* Philomel, 1984. (Objective 1)
Illustrations add visual and sensory excitement to the tale of the busy spider who will not be diverted.

Emberley, Barbara. *Drummer Hoff.* Illustrated by Ed Emberley. Prentice-Hall, 1967. (Objective 1, 3)
Woodcut illustrations enhance the catchy, cumulative rhyme about building and firing a cannon.

Flack, Marjorie. *Ask Mr. Bear.* Macmillan, 1932. (Objectives 1, 2, 3)
Danny asks the animals to give him something for his mother's birthday, and the bear suggests a nice surprise.

Galdone, Paul. *Henny Penny.* Clarion, 1968. (Objective 3)
A less-frightening fox leads the animals on a shortcut to the king in this version of the Chicken Little tale.

Galdone, Paul. *The Three Bears.* Seabury, 1972, op. Clarion, 1985, paper. (Objective 3)
Galdone's illustrations add vigor and humor to the traditional tale.

Rounds, Glen. *I Know an Old Lady Who Swallowed a Fly.* Holiday House, 1990. (Objectives 1, 2)
The old woman swallows a number of animals in this traditional nonsense story and finally dies.

Shaw, Charles G. *It Looked Like Spilt Milk.* Harper & Row, 1947, 1988. (Objectives 1, 4)
A collage of torn paper sometimes looks like something else but is really a cloud in the sky.

Stevens, Janet. *The Three Billy Goats Gruff.* Harcourt Brace Jovanovich, 1987. (Objectives 1, 2)
Despite the troll's threats, the three billy goats cross the bridge.

Tafuri, Nancy. *Have You Seen My Duckling?* Greenwillow, 1984. (Objectives 1, 2, 3)
The baby ducks follow their mother around the pond as she asks other animals if they have seen her lost duckling.

Wood, Audrey. *The Napping House.* Illustrated by Don Wood. Harcourt Brace Jovanovich, 1984. (Objectives 1, 4)
One by one sleepy creatures join a napping scene until a flea causes a disaster.

Zemach, Margot. *The Little Red Hen.* Farrar, Straus & Giroux, 1983. (Objectives 1, 2)
Humorous illustrations extend the appeal of this traditional tale.

GROUP INTRODUCTORY ACTIVITY:

Preparing for the Activity: Locate Charles Shaw's *It Looked Like Spilt Milk.* Also collect a length of string or ribbon for demonstration. Be certain that you have white paper and dark construction paper for the extending activity. If possible, duplicate strips of paper (four or five per page) that say, "Sometimes it looks like a _____ ."

Focus: Show the children a length of thick yarn or ribbon. Say, "Tell me what I can make with this yarn." Demonstrate using it as a belt. Write "Belt" on the board and continue. After each answer, say, "It could be a belt, a necklace, or a bracelet, but it's really a piece of yarn." Generate a list of their suggestions of things that the yarn can be, and write each word on the board as you repeat it. Reinforce divergent answers. While the children are still responding, summarize the list, saying, "Sometimes it looks like...." and read all the words from the board.

Objective: To satisfy the objectives of sharing repeating words and phrases and of writing a parody, introduce Charles Shaw's *It Looked Like Spilt Milk.* Say, "While I read this book to you, your job is to find words that you can read with me. This book will be easy for us to read together."

Guided Activity: Read the book aloud and show the pictures. Pause just before you read the repeating pattern. Point to the words as you read and encourage the children to recite them with you. When a number of the children recognize the pattern, you can simply point to the words as the children recite and you read only the new words on the page. Children will quickly use picture clues to predict the new words. Reinforce all efforts and describe these efforts as "reading." When you finish the book, review the pattern by asking the children to recall an object from the story and repeat the words they remember about the object. Stop while the children are still reciting out loud.

Extending Activity: Give the children white paper to tear, and one piece of dark paper. Let everyone tear the white color into shapes to be glued onto the other color. Label each page with the words, "Sometimes it looks like a _____ ." If a duplicating machine is available, prepare pages with these words before beginning the activity. Let each child identify his or her picture and write the word, or you write the word the child suggests. If necessary, ask older students or an aide to help with the writing.

Form a circle. Let the children read their pages. Then as a group, decide what word will complete the line, "It was just a _____ ." After the teacher completes this page, assemble the pages into a book. Prepare a title page. Ask each child to sign the title page as the author. Place the book on the reading table for children to share. During the year, look for opportunities to use the phrase, "Sometimes it looks like _____ " with the children.

FOLLOW-UP ACTIVITIES FOR TEACHER AND STUDENTS TO SHARE:

1. Read aloud Margaret Wise Brown's *Wait Till the Moon Is Full.* Urge the children to join in as soon as they recognize the repeating phrase, "Wait till the moon is full." Stop before the last page to see if anyone can anticipate the four-word ending. Serve round cookies and see if the children can identify what moon shape the cookies represent. Suggest that the children bite into the cookies and produce a "raccoon's" ear.
2. Read Eric Carle's *The Very Busy Spider.* Tell the children that whenever you point to them, they are to help read the story by repeating the lines, "The spider didn't answer. She was very busy spinning her web." Read the story. As a follow-up, let children make yarn webs.
3. As you read Barbara Emberley's *Drummer Hoff,* pause before reading the last word in each sequence of events so the children can anticipate what every character could be bringing. As the cannon is built and the characters assembled, point to each previous character and let the children chant the lines evidencing previous actions. As a follow-up have children pantomime the action as the teacher reads the text.

4. Read aloud Marjorie Flack's *Ask Mr. Bear*. Before reading the lines, let the students anticipate what Danny will say to each new animal. Children should join in on other repeated lines. After the story is read, see how many repeated lines they can recall. Make felt flannel board characters for Danny and the animals and have the children tell the story as you add characters to the board.

5. Read Paul Galdone's *Henny Penny*. After Cocky Locky asks, "May I go with you, Henny Penny?," stop, and before reading the next lines, let the children anticipate what Ducky Lucky and the rest of the animals will say.

6. Read aloud Paul Galdone's version of *The Three Bears*. While you are reading the story, have the children anticipate what Mother Bear will say each time after Father Bear speaks. Talk about the meaning of the word "porridge." Teach the children the old "Peas Porridge Hot" rhyme. Discuss the repetitive words in the rhyme. Divide the class into pairs who will clap the poem while repeating the lines in unison.

7. Read Glen Rounds' version of *I Know an Old Lady Who Swallowed a Fly* aloud to the class. Let the children join in on the repeating lines of this cumulative tale. Make a felt woman with a large skirt and attach to a large cardboard. Make the felt animals mentioned and place them on the flannel board while the children recite the patterned lines of the story. Sing the song together.

8. Read Janet Stevens' version of *The Three Billy Goats Gruff*. As the story progresses, the children should join in on the sound of the bridge and the words of the troll. At the end of the story, talk about the repeating lines. With a bridge, three goats, and a troll that will fit on the overhead projector stage, let the children retell the story.

9. Read Nancy Tafuri's *Have You Seen My Duckling?* Let the children tell what happens on the pages where there is no narration. As a group have them repeat the mother duck's question. After sharing the story, let the children recall the events and narration, assign parts, and play out the story.

10. Read Audrey Wood's *The Napping House*. Urge children to repeat the lines that identify the sleeping characters as they are added to the tale. Create a new story with the same pattern about a noisy house. Let a mother's saying "Shh" start the quieting that each character continues with the next animal until they all fall asleep. Urge children to be original in the way each is quieted (rubbing its back, singing softly, rocking, etc.).

11. Read aloud Margot Zemach's *The Little Red Hen*. Let the children join in by reciting the chorus "'Not I,' said the _____ _____ " and "'Then I'll do it myself,' said the little red hen." After reading the story, let the children identify the progressive

events from grain to bread. Finish the activity in a memorable way by sharing a loaf of homemade or home-style bread.

Sequencing

STUDENT OBJECTIVES:

1. Relate what happens next in a folktale.
2. Recall major events in stories.
3. Sequence words from an ABC book in alphabetical order.
4. Say the next letter in an ABC book and name an object or word that begins with that letter.

RECOMMENDED READING:

Brown, Marcia. *All Butterflies.* Charles Scribner's Sons, 1974. op., Macmillan, 1981, paper. (Objective 4)
Words for letters of the alphabet paired in succession are illustrated with woodcuts.

Cauley, Lorinda Bryan. *The Pancake Boy.* G. P. Putnam's Sons, 1988. (Objectives 1, 2)
In this unique retelling, the runaway pancake meets Henny Penny, Cocky Locky, and Ducky Lucky before being eaten by the pig.

Ehlert, Lois. *Eating the Alphabet.* Harcourt Brace Jovanovich, 1989. (Objective 4)
Brightly illustrated vegetables and fruits whet the appetite as the reader is invited to eat his or her way through the book.

Freeman, Don. *Rainbow of My Own.* Viking, 1966. (Objective 2)
A little boy plays rainbow games and then finds a rainbow all his own.

Friedrich, Priscilla. *The Easter Bunny That Overslept.* Illustrated by Adrienne Adams. Lothrop, Lee & Shepard, 1965, 1983. (Objective 2)
After oversleeping, the bunny unsuccessfully tries to deliver eggs on other holidays.

Gag, Wanda. *ABC Bunny.* Coward-McCann, 1933, 1961. (Objective 3)
Rhyming text identifies the letters of the alphabet.

Gag, Wanda. *Millions of Cats.* Coward-McCann, 1928, 1977. (Objective 2)
An old man must cope with millions of cats in his efforts to find one for his wife.

Kellogg, Steven. *Chicken Little.* William Morrow, 1985. (Objectives 1, 2)
Illustrations and text modernize the well-known story.

MacDonald, Suse. *Alphabatics.* Bradbury, 1986. (Objectives 3, 4)
As each letter changes position and is given added detail, it becomes an appropriate object.

McCloskey, Robert. *Blueberries for Sal.* Viking, 1948. (Objective 2)
Sal and Little Bear become confused as they pick berries with their mothers.

Ormerod, Jan. *The Story of Chicken Licken.* Lothrop, Lee & Shepard, 1985. (Objectives 1, 2)
Text and illustrations show a group of children presenting the story as a stage play.

Sing a Song of Popcorn. Illustrated by nine Caldecott medalists. Scholastic, 1988. (Objective 1)
A variety of well-known poets are represented in this illustrated collection of 128 poems.

Slobodkina, Esphyr. *Caps for Sale.* Harper & Row, 1947. (Objectives 1, 2)
Monkeys confuse the peddler as they take the caps while he sleeps.

GROUP INTRODUCTORY ACTIVITY:

Preparing for the Activity: Locate Esphyr Slobodkina's *Caps for Sale.* Have a chalkboard or overhead transparency ready on which to write. Allow for space in the room to act the story out. If possible, locate or make paper hats for all the students.

Focus: Ask a volunteer to tell the class how he or she got ready for school today. Tell the children that you want to know everything that happened. After the child's narration, ask if he or she could have left the house before he or she got up. Discuss the fact that there was an order to the things the child did to get ready for school, and that some of the steps had to be in a certain order. Ask if anyone else does things in a different order. Let several children share their routine. Find ways that their orders of events are the same and ways they differ. Tell the children that if they had just been telling stories, some parts of the stories would have happened in different order, but that the end of everyone's story is the same—they all came to school today.

Objective: To satisfy the objectives of relating what happens next in a story and arranging events of a story, say, "The story I'll read to you happens in a certain order, just like your morning stories. As I read this story, listen carefully to what happens in this story, so that you can remember the order." Tell the students to listen to the repeating words in the story. Those words make the story more fun.

Guided Activity: Introduce Slobodkina's *Caps for Sale.* As you read, invite the children to join in when the peddler cries, "Caps for sale," and "Give me back my caps." When you are finished, ask the children to tell you the important parts of the story in order. As they retell, ask questions like "What happened next?" and "Then what?" Ask the class if the details in the retelling are in the same order as in the book. Write a word or phrase on the board or overhead as the children relate a detail. Leave space between episodes in case a detail or episode needs to be added. Repeat the words as you write and relate the sequence, since most children cannot read them independently. Once the story is retold to the class' satisfaction, show the children that the words you wrote are in the same order as the story and can help remind anyone about the story.

Extending Activity: Using the outline prepared by the class, review the sequence of the story. Let the children act out the story, with one child as the peddler and the rest of the class playing the monkeys. If there is a hat for each child, the activity will be more authentic. Since this story involves noise, it may be wise to perform outside or in an area where noise and activity will not bother other classes.

FOLLOW-UP ACTIVITIES FOR TEACHER AND STUDENTS TO SHARE:

1. Before showing the class Marcia Brown's *All Butterflies,* tell them to pay special attention to the illustrations. Explain that these are woodcuts—pictures printed from a block of wood that an artist has cut. After looking together at the book, let the students make up a new ABC book using the letters in succession, making two-word sentences. Start with the example *Animals bite.* Continue with: *Children dance; Ears flop; Giraffes hop.* Assist the children with ideas as needed. Write each combination on a separate page and let the children illustrate the pages. When they have finished let the children make a book by arranging the pages in the correct sequence.
2. Before sharing Lorinda Cauley's *The Pancake Boy,* read Rowena Bennett's poem "The Gingerbread Man" from *Sing a Song of Popcorn.* As the children recall the events of the poem, list their responses on the board. Leave spaces so that they can discuss

proper sequence. Talk about the meaning of words such as "sower" and "reaper."

Now read Cauley's *The Pancake Boy*. Review the blackboard list and have the children talk about the differences in the two versions.

Have children suppose an adult made them a cookie boy. What would they do if it ran away? Using either construction paper or raw cookie dough that will later be baked, let the children make a cookie boy face.

3. Show the class the pages of Lois Ehlert's *Eating the Alphabet*. Before sharing the illustration for each letter, have the children say the next letter and see if they can think of an article of food beginning with each letter. Talk about the taste and preparation of the food illustrated and see if any are unfamiliar to the students.

    As a follow-up, locate at the grocery store an exotic fruit or other item of food unfamiliar to many in the class. Bring it to school and let each child have a taste.

4. Read Don Freeman's *Rainbow of My Own*. Recall the major events in the story. Have the children each wrap a dowel stick with crepe paper of different colors to make a rainbow wand. As you reread the story, the children will wave their wands in an arc whenever the word "rainbow" is mentioned in the story—making rainbows of *their* own.

    Let children suggest games they might play with a pretend rainbow or with their rainbow wands. If there is a prism or goldfish bowl available, perhaps the children can see a rainbow in the classroom.

5. Read Priscilla Friedrich's *The Easter Bunny That Overslept* to the class. Then share the illustrations again and let the children sequence the major events. Are they satisfied with the ending?

    Discuss the other holidays the bunny could have tried that were not described in the story. How would the bunny have decorated the eggs for each of the holidays named? Give the children a paper egg shape and let them decorate it for the holiday of their choice. Arrange them in calendar sequence for an *Easter Bunny That Overslept* bulletin board.

6. Before sharing Wanda Gag's *ABC Bunny* with the class, make 26 cards for the alphabet, writing for each letter the word that Gag used to identify it. Read the book to the class, stopping to let the children try to give the identifying word, using the illustration as their clue. Talk about the meaning of unfamiliar words such as "gale" and "view." Distribute the cards in random order. Reread the book. Have the child holding the appropriate card stand in line and say the identifying word. Others in the class may need to help in remembering the sequence of the alphabet. Teach the class the ABC song.

7. Before reading Wanda Gag's *Millions of Cats*, have the children recall and repeat the nursery rhyme "I love little pussy." Talk about why cats make good pets. Tell the children you are going to read them a story about an old lady who was lonely and wanted a cat for a pet. Remind the children to listen carefully because you are going to ask them afterwards to recall the events of the story in the right order. As you read *Millions of Cats*, urge the children to join in saying the refrain. After reading the story, ask the class to recall the events in sequence. Talk about why the one cat did *not* fight. Suggest they draw a picture of their favorite cat. Display their cats on a *Millions of Cats* bulletin board.

8. Read Steven Kellogg's *Chicken Little* to the class. Have them recall the major events of the story in sequence. Start the story for them and continue with a series of "What happened next?" questions until the entire story is told. Show them the appropriate illustrations to jog their memories as needed.

   On the following day read Jan Ormerod's *The Story of Chicken Licken*. Let the children talk about the differences in the Ormerod and Kellogg versions. Which did they enjoy more? Why? Let the class recall the sequence of events in the Ormerod story and what the characters said. Have the students act out the story, with a different child serving as narrator for each event.

9. As you read Suse MacDonald's *Alphabatics* to the class, use a piece of construction paper to cover the right-hand page depiction of each letter. Let the children see the illustrations of the letter on the left-hand page, observe the changes, and see if they can guess what the object will be before you reveal it. Before you turn to the next letter, let the children anticipate the letter and talk about what the object might be. Continue to cover the right-hand page as you share the book.

10. Read Robert McCloskey's *Blueberries for Sal* to the class. Let children recall the events in the story while you list them on the blackboard. Return to the book as needed if they forget major events. Review the list and talk about what the characters would say as the events unfold. Play out the story. Then let each child either eat a blueberry from a can you brought or sample a piece of blueberry muffin.

Characterization

STUDENT OBJECTIVES:

1. Describe the main character in a story.
2. Compare and contrast character traits with one's own character or with other characters in the story.
3. Identify the changes in characters within a story.
4. Identify and discuss a favorite character in a story.

RECOMMENDED READING:

Aruego, Jose, and Ariane Dewey. *Rockabye Crocodile*. Greenwillow, 1988. (Objective 2)
A kind boar and a selfish boar care for Mrs. Crocodile's baby and are rewarded appropriately.

Brett, Jan. *Annie and the Wild Animals*. Houghton Mifflin, 1985. (Objectives 1, 2)
After Annie's cat disappears, she tries unsuccessfully to find a pet among the woodland animals.

Clements, Andrew. *Big Al*. Illustrated by Yoshi. Picture Book Studio, 1988. (Objective 1)
An ugly but nice big fish has trouble making friends until he rescues the smaller fish from a net.

Freeman, Don. *Corduroy*. Viking, 1968. (Objective 3)
Although his search for his lost button is unsuccessful, the little toy bear acquires a friend.

Graham, Bob. *Crusher Is Coming*. Viking, 1988. (Objective 1)
Pete's plans for entertaining Crusher, the school football hero, go awry as Crusher enjoys entertaining Pete's little sister.

Green, Norma. *The Hole in the Dike*. Illustrated by Eric Carle. Thomas Y. Crowell, 1975. (Objectives 1, 2)
A simply told version of the tale of a courageous boy who saves his country from being flooded.

Jeffers, Susan. *Wild Robin*. E. P. Dutton, 1976. (Objectives 3, 4)
The character of Robin, who hates work, changes when he is kidnapped to fairyland where all he has to do is play.

Keats, Ezra Jack. *Peter's Chair*. Harper & Row, 1967. (Objective 3)
A small boy changes his attitude about the painting of his furniture for his baby sister.

Lionni, Leo. *Frederick.* Pantheon, 1967. (Objectives 1, 2)
A small mouse gathers colors and words as his share of the winter's food.

Piper, Watty. *The Little Engine That Could.* Illustrated by Richard Walz. G. P. Putnam's Sons, 1980. (Objectives 2, 4)
Only the little blue engine will help the broken-down train that is carrying toys and goodies for children.

Steig, William. *Sylvester and the Magic Pebble.* Simon & Schuster, 1969, 1988. (Objectives 1, 3)
Sylvester makes an unwise wish and must wait for someone to help him.

Zolotow, Charlotte. *A Tiger Called Thomas.* Illustrated by Catherine Stock. Lothrop, Lee & Shepard, 1963, 1988. (Objectives 1, 3)
Shy Thomas has difficulty making friends until he is recognized wearing a tiger suit on Halloween.

GROUP INTRODUCTORY ACTIVITY:

Preparing for the Activity: Locate Ezra Jack Keats' *Peter's Chair.* Be certain that there will be an area clear for the children to sit in a circle during the extending activity.

Focus: Ask the children if anyone has a younger brother or sister in the house. Let several talk about their experiences with babies and the changes they bring. Ask, "Do you think the big brother or sister would change much if there were a baby in the family?" Concentrate on the changes an older sibling would experience in this situation—what things would change in the house? What feelings would change inside the older child?

Objective: To satisfy the objective of identifying the changes in characters within a story, tell the children you will read a book about a boy who is a new big brother. Tell them to listen carefully for words that tell how he is feeling and how he changes.

Guided Activity: Introduce Keats' *Peter's Chair.* You can incorporate previous lessons in predicting or visual literacy by asking the children to predict what the story could be about, and by telling them to look for the special ways Keats makes his pictures. Read the story. When finished, ask the children to remember words from the story that tell how Peter is feeling. Find the passages identified and reread them. Focus on the sequence where Peter's feelings are made clear as he first thinks, then whispers, then mutters and shouts. Ask, "What does his chair mean to Peter? Why doesn't he want to share?"
Draw a line down the middle of the board, and label one side, *At first,* and the other, *But then.* Ask the children to tell you the things

that Peter says and does at the beginning of the story. Write these ideas down, and read the passages from the book. Now reread the first idea, and ask if Peter changes his behavior at the end of the story. Continue reading and asking if there is a change in Peter from the beginning to the end of the story. Tell the children that in many stories, a character changes, and as readers, they must watch for change.

Extending Activity: Seat the children in a circle, and tell them that you want them to share something about themselves that makes them like Peter. Suggest that this may be when a friend comes to their house, or it might be a time when they changed—tried something new, learned to do something, or decided something for themselves. Go around the circle, and have each child start by saying, "I changed like Peter did when I . . ." Allow children to pass, but tell them you'll come back to them at the end, and that they will probably have something to share then.

FOLLOW-UP ACTIVITIES FOR TEACHER AND STUDENTS TO SHARE:

1. Read Jose Aruego and Ariane Dewey's *Rockabye Crocodile* to the class. Then let the children compare and contrast the characters of the two boars at the beginning of the story. Which boar do the children like? Why? Let the children pretend the two boars have cared for a little baby who is visiting the classroom. Give them two baskets in which to place things appropriate for each boar. They may want to go out in the schoolyard to collect items. Label the baskets with each boar's name.

2. Before reading Jan Brett's *Annie and the Wild Animals,* tell the students to listen for ways they feel they are alike and different from Annie. When the story is finished, ask the students to recall times when Annie felt lonely. Suggest that she was loyal, that she was independent, and that she was willing to try to solve a problem. Have them document each of these traits with details from the story.

   Let the class discuss how Annie was like and different from each of them. What would they do if a pet were lost or if wild animals came to their home?

   As a follow-up ask the children to suppose that Annie lacked the character trait of loyalty. How would that have changed the story?

3. Read Andrew Clements' *Big Al* to the class. Let the class describe Big Al's physical appearance. Now ask the class to describe his character. If they do not describe Al as polite, sad, lonely, awkward, or with other such adjectives reread pages from the book to give them clues. Why were the little fish afraid of

Big Al at the first of the story? Why were they not afraid at the story's end?

As a follow-up let the children color and cut out little fish and Big Al. Drape a net over the little fish on one side of a bulletin board labeled "Big Al Saved Them."

4. Before reading Don Freeman's *Corduroy* tell the children to think about how Corduroy feels throughout the story. After finishing the story ask the children to describe events that made them know Corduroy was lonely and that he wanted something. What do they think he really wanted? Why would he rather live with the little girl in a small room than in a palace? Why did the little girl want Corduroy even though he didn't look brand new? How did Corduroy change? Urge the children to bring a favorite stuffed animal to class and tell how their animal is like Corduroy.

5. Before reading Bob Graham's *Crusher Is Coming*, let the children discuss how they feel when a friend comes to visit them. Are there any things they want members of the family to do or not do while the friend is there?

Read the story to the class. Then let them discuss what character traits Pete thought Crusher had at the first of the story. What did he want his family not to do? How were Crusher's character traits different from what Pete thought they were? What actions of Crusher showed this? Will Crusher visit again?

6. Read to the class Norma Green's *The Hole in the Dike*. Ask the children to characterize Peter, justifying their ideas with events from the story. Have them discuss whether they feel all children would have been as brave. Why or why not? At the end Peter says he is not a hero. Does the class agree or disagree? What makes a hero?

Tell the children that the story was first written in 1865. Suggest that they go home and tell the story to their parents or another adult. See if the adults remember hearing the story when they were children. Do the adults remember any differences in the version they heard? Give the children time to share their findings with the class.

7. Before reading Susan Jeffers' *Wild Robin,* ask the children to describe chores they do around the house. How do they feel about doing them? After reading the story let children talk about Robin's character traits at the opening of the story. Did he change? Why? Who do the children feel is their favorite character in the story? Why?

8. Before reading Leo Lionni's *Frederick,* ask the children if they have ever formed an opinion of someone and later found they were wrong because they had judged too soon. Read the book to the class. Then let the children discuss how they felt about Frederick at the first of the story. Why did he appear to be lazy?

How was he different from the other mice? Did the class change their minds about Frederick by the end of the story? Why?

As a follow-up duplicate for each member of the class a sheet of paper titled "I like Frederick because . . ." Let them each tear a Frederick from gray paper for the middle of the page. At the bottom of the page the teacher or an adult aide or volunteer can record each child's response to the fragment sentence of why he or she likes Frederick.

9. Read Watty Piper's *The Little Engine That Could* to the class. Have the children discuss the character traits portrayed by each of the engines who were asked to pull the train. Which engine did they like best? Why?

    Play out the story. Let the children who are on the train be a chorus that repeats "I think I can . . ." and "I thought I could . . ." as the little blue engine crosses the mountain.

10. Before reading *Sylvester and the Magic Pebble,* tell the class that this book won the storyteller, William Steig, an important prize, the Caldecott Medal, for his outstanding illustrations. Urge them to look at the pictures carefully as they hear the story, because the illustrations give clues to Sylvester's character.

    After they have heard the story, ask the children to describe Sylvester's character at the beginning of the story. Was he happy? What actions or descriptions helped them decide how he was feeling. What were other character traits? How did they form those impressions? After he became a rock, did any of Sylvester's traits change? Did he change again by the end of the story?

    Why did the family put the magic pebble in an iron safe? What might they use it for someday? Let children discuss what wish they would make if they had a magic pebble.

    Let the class take a walk in the schoolyard or around the block and find a special pebble. Let them paint it their favorite color and put it into a magic pebble display.

11. Read Charlotte Zolotow's *A Tiger Called Thomas.* Have the children characterize Thomas as he was at the first of the story: shy, lonely, etc. Why did he feel that way? Did he change at the end of the story? If so, what made him change? How did Thomas' mother feel at the end of the story?

    As a follow-up suppose that Thomas and his mother plan a "fall fun" party to which they will invite Marie, Gerald, and the other young friends in the neighborhood. Let the children plan the party. What will the invitations say, what games will they play, and what will the refreshments be? Let the class pretend to be Thomas' friends and have the party they planned.

Plot Line

STUDENT OBJECTIVES:

1. Identify the problem in a familiar rhyme or story.
2. Identify the solution to a problem.
3. Give a personal, original solution to a problem in a rhyme or story.
4. Decide if the problem and solution are realistic.

RECOMMENDED READING:

Aseltine, Lorraine. *First Grade Can Wait.* Illustrated by Virginia Wright-Frierson. Albert Whitman, 1988. (Objectives 1, 2)
Luke has mixed feelings about school and going on to first grade until his parents tell him there is another choice.

Bunting, Eve. *The Mother's Day Mice.* Illustrated by Jan Brett. Clarion, 1986. (Objectives 1, 2, 4)
Littlest mouse solves the problem of what to give mother for Mother's Day.

Hedderwick, Mairi. *Katie Morag Delivers the Mail.* Little, Brown, 1988. (Objectives 1, 2, 3, 4)
Katie mixes up the packages she delivers, but her grandmother helps solve the problems caused.

Isadora, Rachel. *The Pirates of Bedford Street.* Greenwillow, 1988. (Objectives 1, 2)
Joey creates exciting scenes on the sidewalk and causes a problem with Mrs. Miller.

James Marshall's Mother Goose. Farrar, Straus & Giroux, 1979. (Objectives 1, 2, 4)
Marshall's clever characters give surprises to the familiar rhymes.

Kraus, Robert. *Leo the Latebloomer.* Illustrated by Jose Aruego. Crowell, 1971, 1987. (Objectives 1, 2)
Although father worries about Leo's problems in learning skills, his mother knows he will bloom.

Le Guin, Ursula K. *A Visit from Dr. Katz.* Illustrated by Ann Barrow. Atheneum, 1988. (Objectives 1, 2, 3)
Marianne feels sick and sorry for herself until mother sends the two cats to distract her from her problems.

Lionni, Leo. *Tillie and the Wall*. Alfred A. Knopf, 1989. (Objectives 1, 2, 3, 4)
By perseverance Tillie satisfies her curiosity about what is on the other side of the wall.

Marshall, James. *George and Martha*. Houghton Mifflin, 1972. (Objectives 1, 2, 3, 4)
Five short stories illustrate the friendship of two hippopotami as they face problems.

Mayer, Mercer. *There's an Alligator Under My Bed*. Dial, 1987. (Objectives 1, 2, 3)
Bedtime is a problem until the little boy lures the alligator into the garage.

Mother Goose. Illustrated by Tasha Tudor. David McKay, 1944, 1980. (Objectives 1, 2)
Illustrations bring a love of the countryside to seventy-seven familiar rhymes.

Payne, Emmy. *Katy No-Pocket*. Illustrated by H.A. Rey. Houghton Mifflin, 1944. (Objectives 1, 2)
A mother kangaroo with no pocket solves the problem of how to carry her baby.

Rockwell, Anne. *Hugo at the Window*. Macmillan, 1988. (Objectives 1, 2)
The dog is lonely and puzzled as he awaits his master's return, but a surprise solves his problem happily.

Tomie de Paola's Mother Goose. G.P. Putnam's Sons, 1985. (Objectives 1, 2, 4)
The rhymes are grouped by topic, and each rhyme is illustrated.

GROUP INTRODUCTORY ACTIVITY:

Preparing for the Activity: Locate *Tomie de Paola's Mother Goose*. Be certain that there is an area large enough for the children to practice and perform their role-playing.

Focus: Recite for the children the nursery rhyme, "Little Bo Peep." Ask, "Why is she sad? What is making her feel bad?" Try to avoid using the word "problem" at this time unless the children introduce it.

Objective: To satisfy the objectives of identifying the problem and solution in a familiar rhyme, introduce *Tomie de Paola's Mother Goose*. Say, "Many of the characters in these rhymes feel bad or sad. Let's see if we can find some."

Guided Activity: Read "Tweedledum and Tweedledee," "Little Poll Parrot," "Rain, Rain, Go Away," "Little Boy Blue," and "Jack Sprat," or any other short rhyme in which the main character has an obvious problem. Ask after each why the character feels unhappy. If by this time no one else has used the word "problem," introduce it. Say, "Let's read another rhyme and see if we can find the problem in it." Read "Three Little Kittens," stanzas 1 and 2. Ask about the problem. Write on the board, "3 Little Kittens." Under, to the left, write *Problem,* leaving room to write *Solution.* Write the problems that the children identify in the rhyme. Read the rest of the rhyme. Ask if the problem gets fixed. How is it fixed? Tell the children that they have just found the solution to the characters' problems. Now write *Solution* on the board to the right and fill in the solution. Say, "In most stories and rhymes, there are problems for the characters, and most of the time, the problems are solved. Next time we read rhymes or stories, let's see if we can find problems and solutions."

Extending Activity: Let the children role-play as nursery rhyme characters. Have them discuss their "problems" with a friend, and suggest ways to solve the problem. Leave this unstructured enough so that the children might begin evaluating the solutions as they appear, and suggesting realistic solutions.

FOLLOW-UP ACTIVITIES FOR TEACHER AND STUDENTS TO SHARE:

1. Before reading Lorraine Aseltine's *First Grade Can Wait* to the class, ask the children if they were worried about going to school or going on to the next grade. Let them discuss why. Tell them that as you read the book, they should listen for Luke's problem, for things that Luke does well, and for things that are hard for him. After reading the story, ask the children to recall the parts of kindergarten that Luke enjoyed. Write *Liked* on the blackboard and record their answers. Then make a *Didn't like* list in the same way. When both lists are done, read them to the class and ask the children why they think Luke feared first grade. Ask how his parents solved the problem. Did Luke feel better then? How do they know?

    As a follow-up, invite a teacher from the next grade to come to your class and chat with the children about activities and expectations of the next grade.

2. After reading Eve Bunting's *The Mother's Day Mice* to the class, have the children identify littlest mouse's problem. What suggestions did the other mice have for solving his problem? What dangers were faced by the mice on their journey? When did littlest mouse get an idea of how to solve his problem? Was it realistic?

    Using the music of "Twinkle, Twinkle Little Star," let the children sing the littlest mouse's Mother's Day song.

3. Read to the class Mairi Hedderwick's *Katie Morag Delivers the Mail.* Let the children talk about the cause of Katie's problem. Did she make a wise decision about a way to solve it? Why or why not? What would have been a better solution? How did grandmother help her solve the problem?

   Let the children think of the contents of four different packages that could have got mixed up. To whom could they have been delivered that could have caused a problem? By what method might the mix-up have been straightened out?

4. Prepare the class for Rachel Isadora's *The Pirates of Bedford Street* by telling them that Joey will make problems for other people without meaning to do so. Ask them to listen carefully for the problem and solution.

   After reading the story, discuss what Joey drew on the sidewalk. Why was Joey's drawing a problem for Mrs. Miller? How do Joey and Mrs. Miller feel about the solution? How do the children know?

   As a follow-up, and with the principal's permission, take the children outside on a warm sunny day. Let them work together to draw a scene they like from *The Pirates of Bedford Street* on a designated portion of the sidewalk.

5. Read "Peter, Peter Pumpkin Eater" from *James Marshall's Mother Goose.* Ask the children to identify the problem in the poem. How did Peter solve his problem? Was it a good idea? Let the children think of some reasons his choice was not a good one.

   Read "Jack Sprat" and "There Once Were Two Cats from Killpenny." Again, analyze the problems, solutions, the realism of the solutions, and other alternatives to the original solutions.

   Leave the book in the reading corner so children can use the illustrations to remind them of other rhymes with problems. Urge them to share the problem and solution with the class.

6. Before sharing Robert Kraus's *Leo the Latebloomer,* have the children identify some skills they have learned that were hard. Ask the children to listen for the problems Leo and his father had in the story. After reading the book, let the children discuss both Leo's and his father's problems. How were they solved? Did Leo's mother have a better solution? Ask what Leo and his father learned in the story.

   Let children recall the skills they earlier identified as hard to learn. Give them a sheet of paper on which has been duplicated, "I was a latebloomer when _____ ." Let the children illustrate a time when they felt like Leo. Complete the caption with their words.

7. Before reading Ursula Le Guin's *A Visit from Dr. Katz,* ask the children if they have ever been ill and had to stay in bed. Did they want to do so? Tell the class that in the story Marianne doesn't want to stay in bed. Ask them to watch for what Mother

did to satisfy her. After sharing the story discuss why Mother had to keep Marianne in bed. What might have happened if she had gone out to play? Were the children surprised at who Dr. Katz was? Have the children discuss how a "Dr. Dog" or "Dr. Canary" could have solved Marianne's problem.

Have the children tell Marianne's story to their parents or another adult. Urge them to ask the adult for stories of how a family pet comforted someone who was sad, frightened, or ill. Let the children share those stories with the class.

8. Read Leo Lionni's *Tillie and the Wall* to the class. Then let children identify Tillie's problem and her efforts to solve it. Where did Tillie get the idea of how to solve the problem? Can the children suggest other solutions? Are theirs as realistic as the one Tillie thought of?

   Tell the children Lionni used collage to make the illustrations. Urge the children to examine the illustrations carefully. Let them make a wall from butcher paper with green construction paper grass at the bottom. Have the children tear or cut paper mice and paste them on the grass as if they were trying to solve the problem by going around the wall.

9. Read the first story "Split Pea Soup" from James Marshall's *George and Martha*. After the story is read let the children discuss the problem and identify the solution. Have children think of other solutions. Was Marshall's solution for George's problem realistic? Why didn't George just tell Martha he didn't like pea soup?

   Read each of the other stories on subsequent days using the same pattern for discussion. On the last day let the children suggest another problem George and Martha may have had as friends; for example, George knocked over Martha's favorite vase and broke it. They may want to share in illustrating the scenes in their simple story. Appropriate words suggested by the children can be written by the teacher under each picture in the sequence.

10. Read Mercer Mayer's *There's an Alligator Under My Bed* to the class. Before reading, tell them to watch the illustrations carefully because watching will help them identify ways the little boy tried to solve the problem. After hearing the story let the class discuss the problem, attempted solutions, and the one that worked. What would the class suggest as possible alligator bait?

    What other things might children imagine to be under the bed? How would they get rid of their fear of each?

11. Select some familiar rhymes from Tasha Tudor's *Mother Goose* that have problems and solutions. Let volunteers act out the rhymes, using the remainder of the class as a chorus each time to say the rhyme aloud. After each verse, have the children identify the problem and the solution. Be sure to use "The Old Woman Who Lived in a Shoe" as Tudor's illustration is not a

traditional one. Ask the children if that is the way they picture the shoe. Discuss the merit of the old woman's solution to the problem.

If videotape equipment is available, the media specialist may want to videotape part of this activity to show to parents at an open house.

12. Read Emmy Payne's *Katy No-Pocket* to the class. Then let children identify Katy's problem and recall the events that led to its solution. Using a Katy No-Pocket puppet (one can be obtained from Beulah's Creations, 2112 Churchill Road, Fort Smith, Arkansas 72904, phone (501) 783-5741) or a flannel board kangaroo and character that can easily be made, let the children take turns telling events in the story that led to the solution. Make the puppet or flannel board available for the children to retell the story in their free time.

13. Share Anne Rockwell's *Hugo at the Window*. Stop to let the children identify Hugo's problem as he first waits at the window. Let children note where the master is on each textless double-spread page. Let children try to anticipate why the master is in the shops. Complete the story. What was the solution to Hugo's problem? Was it a happy one?

What did the lady bring Hugo? Go back through the double-spread pages and see what she did to get ready for the party. If the class had been invited to the party, what would they have taken Hugo as a present?

Vocabulary

STUDENT OBJECTIVES:

1. Identify figurative language in stories and poems.
2. Restate in basic language the message of descriptive words.
3. Create appropriate descriptions or words in stories or rhymes.
4. Define specific words.

RECOMMENDED READING:

Aylesworth, Jim. *One Crow.* Illustrated by Ruth Young. J. B. Lippincott, 1988. (Objective 4)
Counting rhymes show activities on a farm in summer and how they change in winter.

Hayes, Sarah. *Stamp Your Feet.* Illustrated by Toni Goffe. Lothrop, Lee & Shepard, 1988. (Objective 3)
Illustrations suggest actions for variations of traditional nursery rhymes with repetitive language and opportunity to complete lines.

Hoban, Tana. *A Children's Zoo.* Greenwillow, 1985. (Objective 3)
Descriptive words and identification of each animal accompany the color photographs.

Hughes, Shirley. *Out and About.* Lothrop, Lee & Shepard, 1988. (Objectives 1, 3)
Rhyming text and colorful illustrations emphasize the joys of being outside in each season of the year.

Ingpen, Robert. *The Idle Bear.* Bedrick Blackie, 1987. (Objectives 3, 4)
Two teddy bears play with words as they try to find out about each other.

Martin, Bill, Jr., and John Archambault. *Up and Down on the Merry-Go-Round.* Illustrated by Ted Rand. Henry Holt, 1988. (Objectives 1, 2)
Vigorous words and vibrant illustrations evoke the whirl of a carousel ride.

Merriam, Eve. *Blackberry Ink.* Illustrated by Hans Wilhelm. William Morrow, 1985. (Objective 3)
Some of the simple humorous verses in this collection can be chanted as choral poetry.

Peet, Bill. *The Luckiest One of All.* Houghton Mifflin, 1982. (Objectives 1, 2)
The story in rhyme tells of a boy who wishes to be a bird but discovers, when his wishes are granted, that being a boy is best.

Thaler, Mike. *In the Middle of the Puddle.* Illustrated by Bruce Degan. Harper & Row, 1988. (Objective 4)
The rain turns a puddle into an ocean before returning to normal under the watchful eyes of frog and toad.

Tresselt, Alvin. *Hide and Seek Fog.* Illustrated by Roger Duvoisin. Lothrop, Lee & Shepard, 1965. (Objectives 1, 3)
Text and illustrations combine to capture the mood and the spirit of a village enveloped in fog.

Yolen, Jane. *Owl Moon.* Illustrated by John Schoenherr. Philomel, 1987. (Objective 1)
A boy and his father go owling on a winter night.

Zolotow, Charlotte. *Sleepy Book.* Illustrated by Ilse Plume. Harper &
    Row, 1988. (Objective 1)
    Simple text, often using figurative language, extends illustrations
    that show the sleeping habits of a number of animals.

GROUP INTRODUCTORY ACTIVITY:

Preparing for the Activity: Locate Jane Yolen's *Owl Moon* and learn
the finger-play poem. Be certain to have drawing paper, crayons, and
markers for labeling ready for the extending activity.

Focus: Teach the children this finger play:

> Snow comes falling softly down. (Wiggle fingers down.)
> It makes a carpet on the ground. (Smooth fingers flat.)
> Then "whoosh," the wind comes whirling by. (Whirl hands.)
> And the flakes go dancing to the sky. (Wiggle fingers up.)

Repeat the rhyme several times so that all the children can learn
it. Ask, "Can snow really be a carpet? What would a snow carpet feel
like, look like?" Let the children respond and reinforce the responses.
Ask, "What kind of a picture do you think of when you hear the
words 'carpet of snow?'" Draw from the children ideas of flat and
smooth and thick, as well as other images.

Objective: To satisfy the objective of identifying figurative language in
stories, introduce Yolen's *Owl Moon.* Say, "This book has some
beautiful words that make you think of pictures, just like a carpet of
snow. Listen for the beautiful words while I read. I'll ask you to tell
me the words you remember." Before reading, let the children recall a
cold snowy night and how they felt in the cold.

Guided Activity: Read the book and share the pictures. Emphasize the
poetic images as you read. When you are finished, ask the students if
they heard some beautiful words that made a picture in their minds.
If children do recall after one reading, reinforce their listening by
noting that they did a good job. Then say, "I'll read the book again,
and this time we can stop whenever we hear a beautiful word and
we'll save them all on the board." Read again. Pause on the first page
after "statues." Wait for someone to identify that phrase. If no one
does, ask, "What kind of picture do you have in your mind of trees
like statues? These are some of those beautiful words, aren't they?"
Continue to identify and write the phrases on the chalkboard. Allow
time to discuss how the words make the children feel.

Extending Activity: Ask the children to look at all the phrases as you
read from the blackboard list and then have each choose a favorite.
Tell them to pick the word that makes the best picture in their

minds. When everyone has chosen, give the children paper for drawing a picture illustrating the word or phrase. Then help the children label each page with the phrase from the book. Encourage imaginative work. Share each picture with the group and have the children try to guess the phrase from the book. Send the pictures home for the children to share with their families. Close the class with the finger-play and have the children dance like snowflakes.

FOLLOW-UP ACTIVITIES FOR TEACHER AND STUDENTS TO SHARE:

1. Read Jim Aylesworth's *One Crow*. Look back at the summertime activities of the two squirrels, three puppies, and other animals and let the children recall how the winter activities for each group of animals were different. Have the children define the verbs used as you reread them in order to discuss what the animals were doing. Talk about what happens in the four seasons. Let the children use the same animals and create lines for the activities those animals could engage in during the spring and fall. Write their words on overhead transparencies and let children in teams illustrate the lines with water-soluble pens. Let them take turns sharing the words and their illustrations with the class. Assist each with the words as needed.

2. Begin Sarah Hayes' *Stamp Your Feet* by reciting "Pitter-Patter Raindrops." Tell the children you will read the first repetitive phrase in each verse, then you will point to the class to repeat the line you just said. Do not practice. After reciting the entire poem, repeat. Let children decide on appropriate action to play out as they recite.

   Read "The Monster Stomp." Act it out. Then let children think of new actions. Rhyme the lines and decide on a new word the monsters could repeat at the close. This would be an excellent introductory activity for reading Maurice Sendak's *Where the Wild Things Are* (Harper & Row, 1963).

   Many of the rhymes are variations of familiar rhymes. See if the children can recall other versions. Let children compare "I'm a Little Teapot" and "I'm a Little Robot."

3. Share the illustration of each animal in Tana Hoban's *A Children's Zoo* with the class. Have the children identify each animal and think of descriptive words Hoban might have included for each.

   As a follow-up find pictures of farm animals. Let children identify each and think of suitable descriptive words. Include sounds made, the way the animal moves, appearance, etc. Ask volunteers to move like the animals to show the difference between a walk and waddle, for example.

4. Read "Mudlarks" from Shirley Hughes' *Out and About* to the class. Let the children recall all the words describing mud, then think of other appropriate terms. What did the children do in the mud? What other actions could have been included in the poem?

   Read "Spring Greens," letting children suggest the appropriate rhyming word before it is read. Let children study the double-spread illustration that follows in order to suggest other activities that could have been included in the poem. Let children try to add four lines to the poem. Use the same type of activity for each textless double-spread page.

   Read "Sand." What unusual descriptive words were used? Let children think of other descriptive activities related to playing in the sand.

   Read "Squirting Rainbows." Now read it again and have children listen for unusual descriptions and poetic phrases such as "bold as brass." Discuss the meaning. What might the children have said?

   Read "Wind." Notice the words that were used to describe wind and let children think of others. Using the same pattern as "Wind," substitute snow and let children think of appropriate descriptive lines. Write the lines on a large piece of white paper and let children share in illustrating an appropriate border.

5. Read Robert Ingpen's *The Idle Bear* to the class. Go back and from the context let the children discuss the meaning of the words "idle, related, relatives, challenged, annoyed" and "worldly bear." Urge the children to describe what Michael looks like after forty years. Point out that in the final illustration Ted and Teddy are sitting on a dictionary. What else could they have done with the dictionary?

6. Read Dorothy Baruch's poem "Merry-Go-Round," if it is available, as an introduction to *Up and Down on the Merry-Go-Round* by Bill Martin, Jr., and John Archambault. Talk about riding a merry-go-round and think of words that describe the ride. Read Martin and Archambault's book aloud after asking children to listen for and remember words the authors used to capture the excitement. Talk about the words they heard. Did the book's words capture the mood better than the ones the children suggested before the story was read? Reread and have children find places in the book where the words *sound* fast or slow.

   If the story had been about a Ferris wheel ride, how would it have been different? What descriptive and action words might the author have used for a Ferris wheel story?

7. Read aloud Eve Merriam's poem "Latch, Catch" from *Blackberry Ink*. Divide the group in half, assigning one group to say "Latch, Catch" when pointed to and the other to respond with "Come in free." Share the poem as a choral reading. Then have

children think of other things one could catch and add to the poem.

Read the poem "Caterpillar." Have the children think of names of other cities where the butterfly could fly. Write these names on the blackboard and locate on a map. Make new verses for the poem.

Read "Left Foot, Right Foot" as a choral reading. Let children share in making a similar verse with things one could put on hands. Read "Night-light." Let children fill in the rhyming verse at the end of each verse before it is read. Read "Crick! Crack!" Why does the boy have only one mitten to lose? Let children suggest other sounds and fill in rhyming second lines.

8. Introduce Bill Peet's *The Luckiest One of All* by asking the children if they have ever wished to be something else. What did they wish for and why? Read the story to the class, then go back and read the text to them again. This time have the children reword what they would have said instead of "drenched and bedraggled," "cumbersome shell," etc. Talk about why Peet's words are preferable.

Have the children draw a picture of what they might wish to be and make a class book titled "I'd like to be a _____ because _____". The teacher or media specialist can make a caption of each child's response. Encourage children to use descriptive words as Peet did.

9. Read Mike Thaler's *In the Middle of the Puddle* aloud to the class. Urge the children to participate by saying the line "sat a frog named Fred and a turtle named Ted" whenever you point to them during the reading. After the story is completed, have the children recall the bodies of water that the puddles became as the rain continued. Write the suggested words on the board, talk about meaning, and repeat them in order of size.

10. Talk about fog. How do children feel in a fog? Read aloud Alvin Tresselt's *Hide and Seek Fog*. Ask the children to listen for what the afternoon sun turned into, how the sailboats bobbed, how the fog moved past the windows, and how the fog twisted about the cottage. Discuss the descriptive words they noticed. Then reread the story having the children listen for other descriptive words. Have the children generate other words to describe the fog. Write the words on blank paper and allow volunteers to illustrate each particular word or phrase.

11. Introduce Charlotte Zolotow's *Sleepy Book* by asking children how they sleep differently at various times, for example, curled up in sleeping bags when camping out. Suggest they listen carefully to the words that describe each animal's sleeping habits, noting that a sleeping crane looks like a flower on a stem, what spiders look like as they sleep, and what the wind does as the children sleep. Tell them the words make "word pictures" that stay in their minds after the book is closed. Next, read the book

to them and then let the children recall the figurative language you asked them to listen for. In the days that follow, refer to wind that "whispers gently" and spiders that look "like small ink spots in the middle of their lacy webs" to reinforce the impact of descriptive words.

Chapter 2
Second Grade/Third Grade

The skills and strategies identified for the second and third grade level are similar to those for kindergarten through grade 1, except that "Patterns in Literature" is no longer a unit and "Plot Line" has become "Plot/Theme." The objectives for this level are more advanced, and more literary terminology is introduced. Teachers should reinforce students' knowledge and understanding of this terminology by applying it to label concepts whenever possible.

Follow-up activities that demand creative communication skills continue to be an important feature of the units and their use is recommended. Any time students create or write during an extending activity, the teacher should capitalize on the sharing of this product as a way to continue to motivate other students to read and create. If the students have not been introduced to predicting, sequencing, figurative language, and the other basic concepts in previous grades, the teacher may wish to use the relevant activities in the K–T–1 chapter as an introduction to these units.

At this level, able readers can pursue the individual activities independently. Encourage students to attempt these individual activities. Teachers should make every effort to assure that all students have attempted some of the individual activities or suggested follow-ups and shared them with the class.

One new unit has been introduced at this level—nonfiction information books. Students need to be aware that reading expository material calls for strategies different from those used to read fiction. Exploring information will provide motivation for the students who are ready to move from the narrative form of literature into nonfiction.

Visual Literacy

STUDENT OBJECTIVES:

1. Decide why an artist chose a specific medium to illustrate a story.
2. Determine what qualities of a book make its author win the Caldecott Medal.
3. Experience collage, watercolor, oil painting, photography, color pencil, and linoleum blocks as media used in picture books.
4. Compare two picture books illustrating the same story to decide which pictures are more pleasing to the reader.
5. Find small details hidden in illustrations that add humor or understanding to the text.

RECOMMENDED READING:

Ackerman, Karen. *Song and Dance Man.* Illustrated by Stephen Gammell. Alfred A. Knopf, 1988. (Objectives 2, 3)
Grandpa shares with his grandchildren some of the old songs and dances he used to entertain audiences as a vaudeville actor.

Ahlberg, Janet and Allan. *Each Peach Pear Plum.* Viking, 1978. (Objective 5)
Folktale and nursery rhyme characters are hidden in each illustration.

Baker, Jeannie. *Where the Forest Meets the Sea.* Greenwillow, 1987. (Objectives 1, 3)
As they camp in an Australian rain forest, a boy and his father are concerned about the future of their beautiful land.

Grass, Ruth. *Hansel and Gretel.* Illustrated by Winslow Pinney Pels. Scholastic, 1988. (Objective 4)
Recounts the Grimm Brothers' tale of the brother and sister lost in the woods who outwit a wicked witch.

Jonas, Ann. *The Quilt.* Greenwillow, 1984. (Objective 5)
A little girl takes an imaginary trip over the quilt as she searches for her stuffed dog.

Keats, Ezra Jack. *Jennie's Hat.* Harper & Row, 1966. (Objective 3)
Because Jennie was disappointed with her plain hat, her bird friends helped make it fancy.

Lesser, Rika. *Hansel and Gretel.* Illustrated by Paul O. Zelinsky. Dodd, Mead, 1984. (Objective 4)
Oil paintings enhance the mood of the Grimm Brothers' tale of the woodcutter's children who are lost in the woods.

Lionni, Leo. *Alexander and the Wind-Up Mouse.* Pantheon, 1969. (Objective 3)
Because of Alexander's friendship the little wind-up mouse becomes real.

Locker, Thomas. *The Mare on the Hill.* Dial, 1985. (Objectives 1, 3)
Oil paintings intensify the story of the boys who helped an abused mare develop trust again.

McMillan, Bruce. *Growing Colors.* Lothrop, Lee & Shepard, 1988. (Objective 1, 3)
Photography brings alive the colors of a garden and orchard.

O'Neill, Mary. *Hailstones and Halibut Bones.* Illustrated by John Wallner. Doubleday, 1989. (Objective 1)
New illustrations are found in this familiar book of poems about colors.

Pinkwater, Daniel M. *Jolly Roger, a Dog of Hoboken.* Lothrop, Lee & Shepard, 1985. (Objective 1)
Describes how the dog, Jolly Roger, becomes the king of the Hoboken waterfront.

Sing a Song of Popcorn. Compiled by Beatrice S. De Regniers. Illustrated by nine Caldecott Medal winners. Scholastic, 1988. (Objective 3)
The illustrations of nine Caldecott Medal artists enhance this collection of 128 poems by familiar poets.

Thurber, James. *Many Moons.* Illustrated by Louis Slobodkin. Harcourt Brace and World, 1943. (Objectives 1, 2, 3)
Princess Lenore wants the moon and only the court jester can satisfy her wish.

Wolff, Ashley. *The Bells of London.* Dodd, Mead, 1985. (Objectives 1, 3, 5)
The verses of "The Bells of London" are used as a vehicle for the linoleum block illustrations that tell the story of two children who save an escaped dove.

Yorinks, Arthur. *Hey Al.* Illustrated by Richard Egielski. Farrar, Straus & Giroux, 1986. (Objectives 1, 2, 3)
Al and his dog Eddie find that even a life of leisure has its problems.

GROUP INTRODUCTORY ACTIVITY:

Preparing for the Activity: Locate Arthur Yorinks' *Hey Al* as well as *Sing a Song of Popcorn,* illustrated by Caldecott Medal winners. Review the criteria for an artist to be considered for a Caldecott

Medal so that you can lead the discussion. For the extending activity, have watercolors and paper available.

Focus: Ask the children if they know anything about the Caldecott Medal because you will read a winning book to them. After they share, remind them that the Caldecott Medal, named in honor of Randolph J. Caldecott, a nineteenth-century illustrator of children's books, is an annual award given to an illustrator. It is given by the Children's Services Division of the American Library Association to the artist who has illustrated the most distinguished book during the previous year. The criteria that must be exemplified are as follows: The text must be worthy of the book but need not be the work of the artist. The pictures rather than the text are the most important part of the book for this award. The artist must be a citizen or resident of the United States. The book must be published in the United States the year before its award.

Objective: To satisfy the objectives of deciding why an artist chose a specific medium and determining what qualities made a picture book worthy of the Caldecott Medal, tell the student that Richard Egielski won the Caldecott Medal for his watercolor illustrations in Yorinks' *Hey Al*. Suggest that they look carefully at the illustrations so they can determine why this book was selected to win.

Guided Activity: Read Yorinks' *Hey Al*. Give the students time to examine the illustrations. Ask if the illustrations helped to tell the story. If so, in what way? Did the illustrations help the students picture the settings of the book? How does the final illustration help continue the story in the mind of the reader? How will Al's and Eddie's lives be different now? After the class has discussed this book, introduce *Sing a Song of Popcorn*. Explain that all the illustrations in this book were done by Caldecott Medal winners. Read the illustrators' names and see if any of the students know any of the books illustrated by the artists. Share Egielski's illustrations, comparing and contrasting them with his work in *Hey Al*. Ask the students if they see any difference. Ask them to focus on the colors in both books, and how he used them differently.

Extending Activity: Distribute watercolors and paper to the students. Urge them to paint a bird that Al and Eddie might have seen on the island in the sky. Suggest that the students name their birds and write an imaginary description of their size and habits. Label the paintings and display on a bulletin board.

FOLLOW-UP ACTIVITIES FOR TEACHER AND STUDENTS TO SHARE:

1. Before reading Karen Ackerman's *Song and Dance Man,* tell the class that Stephen Gammell won the Caldecott Medal for his color pencil illustrations. After reading the story, ask the children: Did the illustrations help to tell the story? In what way?

   If the children could choose a past profession for their grandfather, what would it be? Have the students use colored pencils to draw their grandfathers working in the job they have chosen.

2. Introduce Janet and Allan Ahlberg's *Each Peach Pear Plum* by telling the class you want them to make a class book titled "I Spy" with fairy-tale characters hidden in the illustrations. To help them get the idea, leave the Ahlbergs' book in the library corner so each member of the class can read the brief text and locate the characters in the illustrations.

   Ask each child to think of a fairy-tale character he or she would like to hide in an illustration. Children should each make one picture and at the bottom of the page write "Find _____ _____ ," naming the hidden character. When all have completed their pictures, place them together into a book titled "I Spy" for the entire class to enjoy.

3. Before reading Baker's *Where the Forest Meets the Sea,* locate the Daintree rain forest on a globe or map. Tell the students the author made two trips there to do research and to collect materials for her relief collages, which she made about the same size as they see in the illustrations. She used modeling clay and the natural materials she found to make the collages.

   After reading the story go through the book again with the class, examining the illustrations in order to identify the countless materials she used. Were these relief collages a good choice for the illustrations? Why or why not?

   If the children were going to make a relief collage to illustrate a park or natural area near their community, what materials would they use? Perhaps they can make a display of some of those materials.

4. In small reading groups have the children share in reading the text of Ann Jonas' *The Quilt.* Have them study the illustrations, watching for the way the girl's imagination changes specific squares of the quilt. What imaginative details does she add when she enters the world of the quilt? How does she leave her imaginary world?

   Have everyone in each group bring a 5-inch square of material from home (the fabric need not be new). Glue the squares together on a paper or white cloth. Now have each group make up an imaginary story involving their squares.

5. Before reading Rika Lesser's version of *Hansel and Gretel,* tell the class that Paul Zelinsky's oil paintings made this a Caldecott Honor book, recognized by the committee for its illustrations, although it did not win the medal.

   Tell the children to study the illustrations as you read the story so they can talk about how the "lost in the forest" scene made them feel. After sharing the story discuss the illustrations, referring to them again as needed. Did the oil paintings help the children imagine that the trees in the forest were actually standing there? How did Hansel and Gretel feel at that time? How did Hansel and Gretel feel in the last scene? In what way did the illustrations change to show that changed feeling?

   On the following day read to the class the Ruth Grass version of *Hansel and Gretel,* illustrated by Winslow Pinney Pels. What was the biggest difference in the text of the two versions? Now discuss the illustrations. Compare Pels' and Zelinsky's illustrations of the "lost in the forest" scene, the witch's house, and the final illustration. Which artist do they feel more effectively illustrated the story? What made them decide this?

6. Before reading Leo Lionni's *Alexander and the Wind-Up Mouse,* tell the class to study the collage illustrations carefully as the book is read, for they will be asked to recall the unusual materials used to compose the collage. After the students identify the materials used, ask them to select a favorite scene. Suggest the class decide on materials and illustrate that scene in a collage mural.

7. Introduce Thomas Locker's *The Mare on the Hill* by asking the class to examine the illustrations carefully. Tell them that after the book is read they will be discussing why they think Locker chose oil painting as the medium for his illustrations. After reading the story, cover the text on the left side of the page and, using the pictures as a guide, let the class retell the story. Have the children discuss their reactions to the oil painting. Why do they think Locker chose oil paint as a medium instead of watercolor, for example?

8. Read some of the poems from Mary O'Neill's *Hailstones and Halibut Bones* to the class. Before reading the second poem let the children suggest items of the same color as that featured in the poem. After sharing some of the colors, ask the class if they feel the illustrations helped them in imagining colors.

   Now tell the class that as you show them McMillan's photographs in *Growing Colors,* they should be thinking about why he chose to use a camera instead of watercolors or some other medium to illustrate his book. Tell them he used a portable water-sprayer on each item before photographing it because he feels that colors in nature are always best when wet with rain.

After examining the illustrations, let the class talk about why they thought photographs were used and why they were effective. If not mentioned, call attention to the impact of the close-up approach.

As a follow-up, let the class take a walk and have each child take a single picture with a 35 mm camera for a book entitled "Colors in Nature." After the film is developed have each child attach the photograph he or she took to a page and write a sentence identifying the object, the color, and stating why that object was chosen.

9. Tell the class to study the pen and ink and watercolor illustrations carefully as you read James Thurber's *Many Moons.* Louis Slobodkin won the Caldecott Medal for the illustrations in 1944.

   After reading the story, talk about the illustrations. Does the class feel Slobodkin would win the Caldecott Medal today? Why or why not? Why do they suppose Slobodkin chose pen and ink and watercolor as his medium?

   Suggest the class members choose a favorite scene from *Many Moons* and, using pen, ink, and watercolor, create an illustration that shows the imaginative approach of the story.

10. Introduce Ashley Wolff's *The Bells of London* to the children by telling them that while the text identifies the churches in the background, Wolff has shared a story of London in the time of Queen Elizabeth. Tell them to observe the illustrations very carefully so that, as a class, they can tell the story.

    Read the book slowly, giving the children time to study the illustrations. Then have the children tell the story of the boy, the girl, and the dove as they share the pictures again.

    Have the children look at one of the illustrations and try to decide what medium was used. After hearing their discussion, tell the class that the illustrations are linoleum block. Suggest that woodcuts were an early medium for illustrations, and linoleum blocks are similar. Let the class decide why Wolff chose this medium instead of color photography, for example. See if the class will conclude that the tale represented was set in early England, so the illustrations should be appropriate for the times. Color photography is a new medium and thus not appropriate.

FOLLOW-UP ACTIVITIES FOR INDIVIDUALS OR SMALL GROUPS:

1. After hearing *Song and Dance Man* by Karen Ackerman, check the school or public library to find other books illustrated by Stephen Gammell. Share your favorite with the class. Are the illustrations similar or different? In what way?

2. Read Ezra Jack Keats' *Jennie's Hat*. Look at the pictures carefully and list the materials used for the collage illustrations. Why was collage a good choice for illustrating the events in the story?

3. Read Ezra Jack Keats' *Jennie's Hat*. At the end of the story what was the only disadvantage to Jennie's hat decorations? Make a large collage illustration of a hat Jennie might have enjoyed wearing.

4. After hearing Thomas Locker's *The Mare on the Hill*, examine the oil paintings again. Choose your favorite illustration and write a short paragraph telling why you made that choice.

5. Read Daniel Pinkwater's *Jolly Roger, a Dog of Hoboken*. On the back of the title page the reader is told that the illustrations were made with an Apple Macintosh computer using the Mac Paint program. Why do you think Pinkwater used a computer to make the pictures? Write a short story about a pet that you have had or one you would like to have. If a computer is available with a program for making pictures, make a computer illustration for your story.

6. After hearing Ashley Wolff's *The Bells of London*, find the nursery rhyme "Polly Put the Kettle On" in the library. Write a short story using the poem as a guide. Be sure to tell why they all went away. Perhaps the teacher or an adult will help you make a potato print border for your story.

Predicting

STUDENT OBJECTIVES:

1. Predict the conflict of a book from the title or first chapter.
2. Predict the plot of a picture book by studying the illustrations.
3. Predict the next chain of events if the author wrote a sequel.
4. Use chapter titles to predict the action of the chapters.
5. Predict the climax of a story.

RECOMMENDED READING:

Allard, Harry. *It's So Nice to Have a Wolf Around the House.* Illustrated by James Marshall. Doubleday, 1977. (Objectives 2, 3)
Cuthbert the wolf is hired by the old man as a companion.

Caudill, Rebecca. *Did You Carry the Flag Today, Charley?* Illustrated by Nancy Grossman. Holt, Rinehart and Winston, 1966. (Objective 1)
In summer school five-year-old Charley finds it hard to be good for a whole day so he can carry the flag at the head of the bus line.

de Paola, Tomie. *Helga's Dowry.* Harcourt Brace Jovanovich, 1977. (Objective 1)
Helga proves herself a clever troll when she earns her own dowry and changes the choice of grooms.

Greenwald, Sheila. *Give Us a Great Big Smile, Rosy Cole.* Little, Brown, 1981. (Objectives 2, 3)
The uncle of untalented ten-year-old Rosy tries to make a book illustrated with photographs that feature her violin-playing.

Haas, Dorothy. *To Catch a Crook.* Clarion, 1988. (Objective 5)
Gabby solves a series of mysteries as part of her research on her Career Day occupation choice: private eye.

Hurwitz, Johanna. *Russell Sprouts.* Illustrated by Lillian Hoban. Morrow, 1987. (Objective 4)
Six-year-old Russell has unusual adventures at home and at school.

Keats, Ezra Jack. *John Henry.* Pantheon, 1965. (Objective 5)
Vivid illustrations highlight the tale of how John Henry races a steam drill.

Lear, Edward. *The Quangle Wangle's Hat.* Illustrated by Helen Oxenbury. Franklin Watts, 1970. (Objective 2)
Well-defined illustrations of the animals clarify the events in Lear's humorous poem.

Lear, Edward. *The Quangle Wangle's Hat.* Illustrated by Janet Stevens. Harcourt Brace Jovanovich, 1988. (Objective 2)
A number of creatures live happily after building their homes on the Quangle Wangle's enormous hat.

Marshall, James. *What's the Matter with Carruthers?* Houghton Mifflin, 1972. (Objectives 1, 5)
The friends of Carruthers, the bear, try to discover why he is so grumpy.

Parish, Peggy. *Good Work, Amelia Bedelia.* Illustrated by Lynn Sweat. Greenwillow, 1976. (Objective 3)
Housekeeper Amelia Bedelia misunderstands directions and carries them out in an amusing way.

Solotareff, Gregoire. *Never Trust an Ogre.* Greenwillow, 1987. (Objectives 1, 5)
An ogre invites the forest animals for dinner and they will *be* the dinner unless an escape plan succeeds.

Van Allsburg, Chris. *The Z Was Zapped.* Houghton Mifflin, 1987. (Objective 2)
A twenty-six-act play results in misfortune for each letter of the alphabet.
Wood, Audrey. *Heckety Peg.* Illustrated by Don Wood. Harcourt Brace Jovanovich, 1987. (Objective 5)
Based on their gift requests a mother recovers her seven children, who have been changed into different foods by the wicked witch.

GROUP INTRODUCTORY ACTIVITY:

Preparing for the Activity: Locate Gregoire Solotareff's *Never Trust an Ogre.* Be near a chalkboard or overhead projector. For the extending activity have writing materials ready.

Focus: Review predicting strategies with the students: making logical guesses, taking risks, and the difference between predicting (when you don't know the outcome) and remembering (because you've read the story and do know the outcome). Ask, "If a cat and a dog were looking at the same piece of meat, what kinds of conflict could you predict?" Review the predictions according to logical guesses.

Objective: To satisfy the objectives of predicting the conflict of a new book from the title and of predicting the climax, tell the students that you have a new book to share. Ask who can tell the class what an ogre is. Be certain that everyone knows how an ogre could be dangerous. Now reveal the title: *Never Trust an Ogre.* Explain that this is a book that has hints about its conflicts in the title. Ask for predictions about the kinds of conflicts that might happen in the book.

Guided Activity: Don't show the cover yet. Ask who might be saying the words of the title. Why should ogres not be trusted? What kinds of problems could someone have with an ogre? Record all the predictions on the board or overhead. Ask the class if the predictions are logical. After you have written the predictions, tell the children that they have used their knowledge of ogres and stories to create several logical conflicts. Now that their predictions are recorded, tell them to listen to the story.

Begin to read. Stop after the ogre sharpens his knife. Ask the students to predict what might happen next. Continue, and stop again after the rabbit says, "I hope you're right." Allow time for students to offer predictions again. Continue, and have them check if their logical predictions match the author's ideas. Stop for the last time when the frogs see the ogre's hunting knife. Ask the class to predict if and how the animals will escape. Then finish the story.

Return to the original predictions of conflict and have the students evaluate each based on the story.

Extending Activity: Ask the students which character might be speaking in the title, *Never Trust an Ogre*. Ask whom we care about, whom we feel sorry for, and whom we want to win the conflict in that title. Now tell the class, "Suppose the title was *Never Trust the Animals*. If the ogre were the hero of the story, how would our ideas of the conflicts change? Could there be other conflicts?" Let the students brainstorm possible conflicts. Then have them write their version of *Never Trust the Animals*. Invite students to write in groups if they desire. Illustrations may be included.

Collect students' writings so that they can read one another's work.

FOLLOW-UP ACTIVITIES FOR TEACHER AND STUDENTS TO SHARE:

1. Cover the words on the opposite page and show the class the illustrations in Harry Allard's book *It's So Nice to Have a Wolf Around the House*. Let the students predict the plot. Then read the story. Were any of the predicted events a part of the action recorded by Allard?

   Predict a series of events that will happen to the characters in Arizona. Have the children illustrate a favorite new event.

2. Before reading the first chapter of Rebecca Caudill's *Did You Carry the Flag Today, Charley?*, explain to the class that the town and school described by Caudill are very different from theirs. They will have to think about the setting in order to predict what will happen. After reading the chapter, discuss the differences between Charley's school and that of the class. Then let the children predict whether Charley will carry the flag that day. Urge them to justify their responses. Suggest that class members check out the book and complete the story and an individual activity. After several have read the story and completed a suggested activity, call the group together and let them share their responses.

3. Read the title and subtitle of Tomie de Paola's *Helga's Dowry*. Explain what "dowry" means and ask for predictions about the main conflict in the story. Read the story to see if the predictions were logical. Have the students identify the conflict between Helga and Lars, Helga and Inge, and Lars and himself.

4. Read the first part of Chapter 1 of Greenwald's *Give Us a Great Big Smile, Rosy Cole*. Stop as the description of Read School begins. Let the class discuss the conflict. Show the class the line drawings in the book and see if they can predict the plot. Suggest they read the book to see if their predictions are correct. Ask each of those who read the book to list predictions of a personal chain of events if Uncle Ralph wanted to do a photographic story of them.

5. Introduce Dorothy Haas' *To Catch a Crook* by saying that this is a Career Day adventure. Gabby decides she will choose "private eye" for her career report and advertises for mysteries to solve. On this and the subsequent two days read to page 79, where Gabby has put together all the notes that she believes are clues. Before reading Chapter 12, ask the students to write their predictions of the solution of the mystery and what will happen on Career Day. Assist any children who have difficulty writing down their thoughts. After they turn in their predictions, read the rest of the story.

   When the story is completed let the children share the predictions and identify the clues they used to try to solve the mystery.

6. Before reading the first chapter of *Russell Sprouts* by Johanna Hurwitz, let the class predict from the title what the story is about. Read the title of the first chapter and let the class predict that chapter. Read the chapter. Continue to have the class predict events from the chapter titles before reading each one.

7. Read Ezra Jack Keats' *John Henry*. Stop as John Henry begins to race the steam drill. Ask the class to predict the climax and justify their decision based on the events thus far. Complete the story. Did anyone predict he would die as soon as he won?

8. To introduce Edward Lear's *The Quangle Wangle's Hat,* illustrated by Janet Stevens, explain to the class that you are going to show them the illustrations but cover up the words and see if they can predict the plot of the poem. After sharing the pictures, let the class discuss the plot. Then read Lear's words as they see the illustrations again. Were any parts of their predictions accurate? Tell the class there is another illustrated version of the poem on the library table. Suggest they read it and complete the individual activity.

9. Show the class James Marshall's *What's the Matter with Carruthers?* Let them predict the conflict in the story from the title. List their predictions on the board. Read the story to page 29 and let the class predict now what is bothering Carruthers. Complete the story. Turn to the students' predictions recorded on the board. Let the class select a favorite conflict idea and as a group decide on the events in the plot and the climax for their story.

10. Introduce Chris Van Allsburg's *The Z Was Zapped* by telling the students to imagine an alphabet theater in which the twenty-six characters meet with misfortune, one by one. Show them the first illustration and let them predict what is happening. Remind them that the first character is an A and the misfortune must also use that letter. Continue through the series of events, letter by letter, giving the class an opportunity to study the illustration and predict the mishap.

After completing the story, suggest the class make a new alphabet play, a twenty-six-ring circus in which good things happen to the alphabet characters or else they perform an enjoyable activity for the audience. Ask each to select a letter. If they wish, they can work together in small groups to figure out appropriate characters and actions to act out. Then have them pantomime in alphabetical order for the rest of the class to guess.

11. Before reading Audrey Wood's *Heckety Peg* tell the children to observe the oil painting illustrations by Don Wood, and listen to the words carefully because you are going to ask them to predict the climax. Read the story to the class. When you reach the page on which the mother looks at the table and identifies the children, go back and review the children's requests for gifts. Now cover the text to the right of the illustration of the table. Have the children predict which child is which item of food by associating the requests (for example, bread and butter). Now read the covered page and complete the story.

Tell the class that Don and Audrey Wood are husband and wife. Discuss the advantages of a married couple working together on a picture book.

FOLLOW-UP ACTIVITIES FOR INDIVIDUALS OR SMALL GROUPS:

1. Select Rebecca Caudill's *Did You Carry the Flag Today, Charley?* Before reading Chapter 2, look at the illustrations in the chapter and write down your prediction of whether Charley will or will not carry the flag that day. Justify your answer. Read the book.

2. Read Rebecca Caudill's *Did You Carry the Flag Today, Charley?* Then go back and name each chapter in a way that would help readers predict what is going to happen. Do not use more than seven words in each chapter title.

3. Imagine Johanna Hurwitz, the author of *Russell Sprouts*, is going to write one more chapter for the story. Remembering events in the book, write down your predictions of the title of the new chapter and what the major events might be.

4. Read Edward Lear's *The Quangle Wangle's Hat* with illustrations by Helen Oxenbury. Study the illustrations. Could you have predicted the plot of the poem more easily if the teacher had shown you *this* book instead of the book with the same poem illustrated by Janet Stevens. Why or why not? Write your answer.

5. Read Peggy Parish's *Good Work, Amelia Bedelia.* Write down a new problem that Amelia Bedelia could cause by misunderstanding instructions.

Sequencing

STUDENT OBJECTIVES:

1. Identify the sequence of events in a narrative poem.
2. Justify why one event must precede another in a story.
3. Arrange events from a story in an appropriate sequence.
4. Sequence events that could happen.

RECOMMENDED READING:

Brett, Jan. *The First Dog.* Harcourt Brace Jovanovich, 1988. (Objectives 3, 4)
   After Paleowolf saves the life of Kip, the cave boy, Kip is happy to share his food and his companionship.

Frost, Robert. *Stopping by Woods on a Snowy Evening.* Illustrated by Susan Jeffers. E. P. Dutton, 1978. (Objective 1)
   Striking illustrations create a story from Frost's familiar poem.

Hoguet, Susan Ramsey. *I Unpacked My Grandmother's Trunk.* E. P. Dutton, 1983. (Objective 3)
   Illustrations inviting participation reinforce the text of the old game in which objects beginning with the letters of the alphabet are taken from the trunk in sequence.

Jacobs, Howard, ed. *Cajun Night Before Christmas.* Illustrated by James Rice. Pelican, 1974. (Objective 1)
   The Louisiana bayou is the setting for this humorous version of Clement Moore's poem.

Kuskin, Karla. *Dogs and Dragons, Trees and Dreams.* Harper & Row, 1980. (Objective 1)
   Imaginative poems are prefaced by short introductory notes about poetry writing and enjoyment.

Leedy, Loreen. *The Bunny Play.* Holiday House, 1988. (Objectives 2, 3)
   The bunnies produce a musical version of *Little Red Riding Hood,* following all the steps in production.

Lexau, Joan M. *I Should Have Stayed in Bed.* Illustrated by Syd Hoff. Harper & Row, 1965. (Objective 3)
   Everything went wrong for Sam and he knew he should have stayed in bed.

Macaulay, David. *Why the Chicken Crossed the Road.* Houghton Mifflin, 1987. (Objective 3)
Illustrations and text record the humorous series of events caused by a chicken who crosses the road.

Moore, Clement. *The Night Before Christmas.* Illustrated by Tomie de Paola. Holiday House, 1980. (Objectives 1, 2)
Tomie de Paola's illustrations enhance the reader's enjoyment of the familiar poem.

Rogasky, Barbara. *Rapunzel.* Illustrated by Trina Schart Hyman. Holiday House, 1982. (Objective 3)
Bordered illustrations add to this appealing version of the Grimm Brothers' tale.

Shura, Mary Francis. *Chester.* Illustrated by Susan Swan. Dodd, Mead, 1980. (Objective 3)
One new boy changes the entire neighborhood in a single week.

Silverstein, Shel. *A Light in the Attic.* Harper & Row, 1981. (Objectives 1, 2, 3)
Humorous verses for all ages are enhanced by the poet's own line drawings.

Stevenson, James. *The Night After Christmas.* Greenwillow Books, 1981. (Objective 4)
A dog helps the doll and teddy bear, tossed in the trash after the children received new toys, to find new homes.

Thayer, Ernest Lawrence. *Casey at the Bat.* Illustrated by Paul Frame. Prentice-Hall, 1964. (Objectives 1, 2)
A proud batter for the Mudville baseball team disappoints the fans when he strikes out.

Thayer, Ernest Lawrence. *Casey at the Bat.* Illustrated by Patricia Polacco. G. P. Putnam's Sons, 1988. (Objective 1)
Text has been added to the familiar poem to give it a Little League application.

GROUP INTRODUCTORY ACTIVITY:

Preparing for the Activity: Locate Silverstein's *A Light in the Attic* and prepare to read "Little Abigail and the Beautiful Pony," page 120, and "Ladies First," page 148. Have another copy of the book for the extending activity, paper for all students, and space to divide the class into two groups. Bring to class a jar of peanut butter, bread, and a knife.

Focus: Show the students the peanut butter, the knife, and the bread. Tell them that you will prepare a peanut butter sandwich in the exact steps that they tell you. Give them time so each student can write the steps on a piece of scrap paper. Ask a volunteer to read the directions he or she has written. Follow the instructions. Ask questions that lead the class to identify all the steps in the correct sequence if the volunteer has left out a step or confused the order. Choose someone to eat your product. Discuss why the order of the steps is important. Introduce the term "sequence" to mean the order of events.

Objective: To satisfy the objectives of identifying the sequence of events in a narrative poem, arranging the events into a sequence, and justifying why one event must precede another, explain that the poems you will read are narrative poems. They tell a story and have a sequence of events. Ask the class to listen for the sequence and be ready to tell why one event must come before another.

Guided Activity: Read Shel Silverstein's poem "Little Abigail and the Beautiful Pony." Have the students recall the sequence of the events. Write the events on the board in the correct sequence. When the class has identified major events, pick any two, and ask why one must come before another. For example, why must Abigail see the pony before she goes to bed? Continue with two or three more examples, selecting two events from the board and asking why one must precede the other. Return to the book, and read two lines of dialogue. Ask which line was spoken first and how the students knew this.

Read the poem "Ladies First." Arrange the details from the jungle trip into proper sequence. Ask why we must know about Pamela's favorite saying before she goes into the jungle. What clues about "Fry-'Em-Up-Dan" does Silverstein include in the poem before Pamela's last line? Why do these details add to the humor of her line? Reread, and ask students to sequence Pamela's demands each time she says, "Ladies first"?

Extending Activity: As a follow-up, divide the class into two groups—an Abigail group and a Pamela group. Let each group reread the appropriate poem and have each student choose his or her favorite line from the poem to copy on a piece of paper. Ask the students to illustrate their line. In their group, using the complete poem, have the students arrange their pictures and lines into the proper sequence. Let the groups design a cover page and share with the other group.

FOLLOW-UP ACTIVITIES FOR TEACHER AND STUDENTS TO SHARE:

1. Read Jan Brett's *The First Dog* to the class. Then let the class recall the sequence of senses Paleowolf used to save Kip. Have the class think of another event that could belong to the sequence, but using another sense. In which order of events would the new idea most logically fit?

Put butcher paper on the board and let the class illustrate their new event. Urge them to examine Brett's borders and make a border appropriate to Paleolithic times to complete their illustrations.

2. Put the lines to Robert Frost's *Stopping by Woods on a Snowy Evening* on a transparency and let the children read it with you. Ask them if the poem tells a story. If they feel it does, ask them to identify the events they feel make up the story.

   Now share Susan Jeffers' illustrated version of the poem. Urge the class to study the illustrations very carefully as you read. They may be able to find a story in her illustrations. After sharing the poem discuss the events illustrated by Jeffers.

3. Introduce Susan Ramsey Hoguet's *I Unpacked My Grandmother's Trunk* by asking if anyone has ever played a game in which you must remember the sequence of events or the words repeated by previous players. Tell the class that they will play such a game with a book. Read the story, having the class guess each item that is in the trunk as well as what will come next. After sharing the book, read or tell the directions for playing the game. Have the class play it, creating new words in alphabetical order rather than remembering those named in the story.

4. Read the poem "Hughbert and the Glue" from Karla Kuskin's *Dogs and Dragons, Trees and Dreams* to the class. Have the children recall the sequence of events in the story. If they had watched these events, how would they have reacted? What was the climax to the poem? What might have been a different climax?

   Read Kuskin's "I Woke Up this Morning." Have the children recall the actions for which the child was criticized. What was the climax of the poem?

   If it is available in the library or through interlibrary loan, show the sound filmstrip *Poetry Explained by Karla Kuskin* (Weston Woods, 1980). Did Kuskin's reading of the two poems the class had already heard increase their enjoyment?

   Suggest to the students that Joan Lexau's *I Should Have Stayed in Bed* will remind them of "I Woke Up this Morning." Suggest they read Lexau's story and do an individual activity related to it.

5. Introduce Loreen Leedy's *The Bunny Play* by asking the class to listen carefully for the sequence of events in producing a play. Perhaps, if they wish to accept all responsibility, they would like to produce a play as a class project.

   After reading the story, ask the class to recall the sequence of events so that you can list on the board the steps in producing a play. As the list grows, let the class justify the appropriateness of the sequence Leedy gives.

   Let the class select a play (perhaps *Little Red Riding Hood*) that they could produce for another class. Talk about the meaning of the words in the glossary. Discuss the roles of those needed to produce a play (director, costume makers, etc.) Produce the play the class plans, being sure all members of the class have a responsibility.

6. Read David Macaulay's *Why the Chicken Crossed the Road* to the class just for enjoyment of the humorous situation. Now go back and read the story again so they can sequence the events. Many events are recorded in the illustrations only, so the class will need to be observant. Let the children answer why the chicken crossed the road.

7. Before reading Clement Moore's *The Night Before Christmas,* have the children try to recall the events of the poem in sequence. Record their responses. Now read the poem. Do they need to add events that they did not remember? Add the new responses and review the events. Why was that sequence necessary?

   Now read Howard Jacobs' *Cajun Night Before Christmas.* How is the sequence of events different in this version? How does the class describe this version? When the class suggests "funny," ask the children what made the poem funny. Was it the events themselves?

   Let the class suppose they were writing a version of the poem for the area in which they live. Describe the sequence of events that might result. They may want to illustrate their version in a textless picture book.

   Show the class James Stevenson's *The Night After Christmas.* Tell them that it will be on the library table. Suggest they may want to read it and complete an individual activity.

8. Before reading Barbara Rogasky's version of *Rapunzel* to the class, suggest that they observe the illustrations carefully. That will assist them as they go back and sequence the events of the story. After reading the story, share the illustrations again and record the list of events given by the class in appropriate sequence.

   Suggest that some students may want to go to the library and find another version of *Rapunzel* to read. Have students who do so refer to the list of events made from the Rogasky version and record any changes. When all who wish to do so have completed this follow-up, let them meet to share their findings.

9. Before reading aloud Ernest Thayer's humorous poem, *Casey at the Bat,* illustrated by Paul Frame, tell the class the history of the poem given in the book. Ask if the students know any famous baseball players who often hit home runs. How does the crowd react when such a player comes up to bat? What does the crowd often do when the umpire calls a strike? Read the poem. Then let the class recall the events in proper sequence. Why was

that sequence necessary for the plot of the poem? What is the class' favorite scene?

The next day read Thayer's *Casey at the Bat* illustrated by Patricia Polacco. List the new events that have been added. Did those events make the class enjoy the poem more? Why or why not? Suggest that a group of students may want to review the Polacco version. Have them plan to act it out for the rest of the class or for another class. If another class is invited, the class may want to serve popcorn to the audience who are participating in the play by being baseball fans attending the game.

FOLLOW-UP ACTIVITIES FOR INDIVIDUALS OR SMALL GROUPS:

1. Read again Susan Jeffers' version of Robert Frost's poem, *Stopping by Woods on a Snowy Evening*. Suppose you were illustrating the poem. Describe the illustrations you would use for the lines to make the story you imagine.
2. Read Joan Lexau's *I Should Have Stayed in Bed*. Record eight events in sequence that helped Sam realize he should have stayed in bed.
3. Read Joan Lexau's *I Should Have Stayed in Bed*. Think of a plot that might make *you* decide *you* should have stayed in bed. List the major events in your plot in sequence. You may want to illustrate those events and make them into a book, using your list of major events as a guide for your simple text.
4. Read again David Macaulay's *Why the Chicken Crossed the Road*. Suppose the title of the story were "Why the Cow Crossed the Road." Think of a series of events that might come from the new title. Be sure the final event answers the question "Why?"
5. Read Mary Francis Shura's *Chester*. The titles of the chapters are the days of the week. Rename the chapters to show the major events that happened in that chapter.
6. Read James Stevenson's *The Night After Christmas*. This story is told by the toys. Think of a sequence of events that might happen if the story were told by a child who threw away either Teddy or Annie.

Characterization

STUDENT OBJECTIVES:

1. Distinguish a round or flat character in a story.
2. Identify static and dynamic characters and explain how that decision was reached.
3. Document how the reader learns about a character from words, actions, and illustrations.
4. Identify traits that make the reader like or dislike a character.

RECOMMENDED READING:

Aylesworth, Jim. *Hanna's Hog*. Illustrated by Glen Rounds. Atheneum, 1988. (Objective 4)
Hanna thwarts the thieving neighbor who steals her hog.

Blades, Ann. *Mary of Mile 18*. Tundra, 1971. (Objectives 3, 4)
Mary finds happiness as the wolf pup earns his keep and can stay in the family.

Cleary, Beverly. *Ramona the Pest*. Illustrated by Louis Darling. William Morrow, 1968. (Objectives 1, 3, 4)
Ramona's enthusiastic approach to life earns her the label "pest" from her older sister Beezus.

Cohen, Caron Lee. *The Mud Pony*. Illustrated by Shonto Begay. Scholastic, 1988. (Objectives 1, 3)
A poor Indian boy becomes a chief with the help of his mud pony, made real by Mother Earth.

Herman, Charlotte. *Millie Cooper, 3B*. Illustrated by Helen Cogancherry. E. P. Dutton, 1985. (Objectives 1, 4)
As Millie faces third grade problems, she discovers new things about her character.

Hoban, Russell. *Dinner at Alberta's*. Illustrated by James Marshall. Thomas Y. Crowell, 1975. (Objectives 1, 2)
Arthur Crocodile learns table manners in order to impress his sister's friend.

Hurwitz, Johanna. *Class Clown*. Illustrated by Sheila Hamanaka. William Morrow, 1987. (Objective 2)
Lucas, a third grader, has difficulties trying to improve his conduct at school.

Kellogg, Steven. *The Island of the Skog.* Dial, 1973. (Objectives 1, 2, 3)
  The mice and one skog learn a lesson about living together in harmony.

MacLachlan, Patricia. *Seven Kisses in a Row.* Illustrated by Maria Pia Marrella. Harper & Row, 1983. (Objectives 1, 2, 3)
  Emma learns to accept the way other people do things as her aunt and uncle stay with her and her brother in their parents' absence.

Ness, Evaline. *Sam, Bangs and Moonshine.* Holt, Rinehart and Winston, 1966. (Objectives 1, 2)
  A near tragedy caused by Samantha makes her discover the difference between real and moonshine.

Parish, Peggy. *Amelia Bedelia Helps Out.* Illustrated by Lynn Sweat. Greenwillow, 1979. (Objective 4)
  Amelia Bedelia and Effie Lou try to do just as Miss Emma says as they "steak" the bean plants and "sew" the grass.

Yashima, Taro. *Crow Boy.* Viking, 1955. (Objectives 1, 2)
  With Mr. Isobe's help the Japanese schoolchildren get new insights into Chibi's character.

GROUP INTRODUCTORY ACTIVITY:

Preparing for the Activity: Locate Steven Kellogg's *The Island of the Skog.* Ask each student to bring one plastic soda bottle to class, or provide them for the students. Have one piece of paper for each student.

Focus: Have the students think of a good friend. Ask the following questions as they think of their friend: What do you like about your friend? How does your friend act? What kinds of things does your friend do and say? Has your friend ever changed the way he or she acted because of something he or she learned? Let the students discuss their friends. Focus on the large number of details the students are able to identify because they know their friends well. Ask about times when their friends changed their behavior, and why.

Objective: To satisfy the objectives of identifying round, flat, static, and dynamic characters and documenting how readers learn about characters, tell the students that characters in a book are like friends—if we listen to them and read carefully, we can learn much. Sometimes characters change the way they act because of what happens to them in the story. Tell the students that you will ask about the characters in this book, and if any of them change.

Guided Activity: Introduce Kellogg's *The Island of the Skog,* telling the students to listen carefully for clues about Bouncer, Jenny, and the Skog. Read the book aloud, allowing plenty of time for the students to enjoy the intricate illustrations.

Discuss the three characters. Ask specifically about what each says and does. Point out to students how often Bouncer snaps and cries—What do these words tell about him? Lead the students to the dialogue, showing how each character's words demonstrate attitudes and feelings. After their discussion of traits, point out that the three are round characters. Ask how much they know about Bouncer, Jenny, and the Skog compared to the other characters in the book. The reader knows little about the other characters so they are flat.

Ask the students to tell you how Bouncer and the Skog change in the story. Have them use the statement, "At first he was _____ ; then he was _____ ." Ask the students to explain why the characters changed. What did the characters learn? Have the students explain why Jenny doesn't change in the same way. Introduce the terms "static" to describe Jenny, whose character shows no change, and "dynamic" to describe the characters of Bouncer and the Skog, which do change.

Extending Activity: Ask the students to pretend that they are stranded with the mice on the Island of the Skog or on the "Flying Rose." Ask what kind of message they would write to put into a bottle for the rest of the world. Give the students a piece of paper and a plastic bottle. Let them crumple and tear the corners of the paper to give the appearance of a scrap of paper. Tell them each to write a message and then roll the paper to put it into a bottle. Display the bottles and allow the students time to read each other's messages inside them.

FOLLOW-UP ACTIVITIES FOR TEACHER AND STUDENTS TO SHARE:

1. Before reading Ann Blades' *Mary of Mile 18,* tell the children that Mile 18 is a real place in Canada where Ann Blades taught in 1971, and the story describes the life of her pupils. After reading the story, have children discuss and document from the story the character traits of Mary that made them admire her. Did the illustrations help them understand Mary? If so, in what way? Discuss with the children ways in which the setting affected Mary's character. Would they like to move with their family to Mile 18?

2. Read to the class the first chapter of Beverly Cleary's *Ramona the Pest.* Then let the class discuss why Beezus thinks Ramona is a pest. Document the character traits of Ramona revealed in the first chapter. Is she a round character? What was the most humorous incident in which Ramona was involved? Suggest that

members of the class read the rest of the story and complete an individual activity.

3. Read Caron Cohen's *The Mud Pony.* Let the children discuss the round and flat characters in the story. How did the reader learn about the Indian boy's character? As a follow-up activity have each member of the class make a clay pony for a Mud Pony display.

4. Before reading Russell Hoban's *Dinner at Alberta's,* talk about actions some people do to impress others. After reading the story let the class discuss whether Arthur was a round or flat character. What traits do we know he had? Did he change and become a dynamic character? Have children document their responses from the story. What happened to Sidney at the tree house? As a follow-up have the students create dialogue and act out table manners, both bad and proper.

5. Before reading Patricia MacLachlan's *Seven Kisses in a Row,* make columns on the board with headings of *Name of character, Character traits,* and *Any changes in character.* Read two or three short chapters. Then let the class begin to offer ideas to fill the columns in the chart. Be sure they document what made them decide to suggest a particular trait. Continue reading the next day and add to or make changes in the chart. Complete the story and the chart on the third day. Let the class identify round or flat, static or dynamic characters. Ask each child to write a short paragraph beginning with "My favorite character in *Seven Kisses in a Row* was _____ because. . . . "

6. Before reading Evaline Ness' *Sam, Bangs and Moonshine* to the class, suggest that they look at the illustrations very carefully to obtain added clues to the character of Samantha. After completing the story, let the students document Samantha's character as round or flat in the story. What traits helped them decide? Did she change and thus become a dynamic character? If so, how and why? If she changed, will it last? Was Thomas a round character? What does the class know about him? Did Thomas change? If not, then he is a static character. Why did Samantha make up Moonshine?

7. Introduce Taro Yashima's *Crow Boy* by describing the school in Japan that is the setting for the story. Suggest that the students read Yashima's *Crow Boy* in order to participate in a group discussion. Urge them to study the illustrations as well as reading the brief text, as that will extend their understanding of the story.

   After the interested students have read the story, focus the discussion on characterization. Was Chibi a round character? Have children document from the story the traits they identify for Chibi. Did Chibi change at the end of the story, making him a dynamic character?

Were the characters of other children round or flat? Did they change or did they remain static? Ask the group to think of how different actions by one child in the school could have changed the events in the story.

FOLLOW-UP ACTIVITIES FOR INDIVIDUALS OR SMALL GROUPS:

1. Read Jim Aylesworth's *Hanna's Hog.* List two things Kenny said, two things Kenny did, and one illustration that made you decide you liked or disliked Kenny.
2. Read Jim Aylesworth's *Hanna's Hog.* List two things Hanna said, two things Hanna did, and one illustration that made you decide you liked or disliked Hanna.
3. Read Beverly Cleary's *Ramona the Pest.* List three of the funniest scenes in the story and name the character trait of Ramona that you can decide upon from reading each scene. Would you like to have her for a sister? Why or why not?
4. As you read Charlotte Herman's *Millie Cooper, 3B,* remember that Herman says many incidents in the story actually happened to her over forty years ago. After reading the story, write a description of Millie's character traits. Is she a round or flat character? If you were an author, what would be the advantage of writing about things that happened to you?
5. Read Johanna Hurwitz's *Class Clown.* Write an answer to the following questions. Why did the author decide on this title? Did Lucas change, becoming a dynamic character? If he did change, how and why did he do so? Would you like to have Lucas for a classmate? Why or why not?
6. Read Peggy Parish's *Amelia Bedelia Helps Out.* What character traits made you like or dislike Amelia Bedelia? For one trait you list, give an event from the story that made you list it.

Plot/Theme

STUDENT OBJECTIVES:

1. Identify rising action that leads to the climax of a story.
2. Note the climax of a story.
3. Identify the conflict in a story or poem.

4. Express the theme of a story.
5. Create a sequel to a story that keeps the same theme.
6. Create a different climax for a story.
7. Understand the meaning of foreshadowing.

RECOMMENDED READING:

Baker, Olaf. *Where the Buffaloes Begin.* Illustrated by Stephen Gammell. Frederick Warne, 1981. (Objectives 4, 7)
   Little Wolf goes out to see the beginning of the buffaloes at the sacred lake and in so doing saves his tribe from attack.
Bang, Molly. *Dawn.* William Morrow, 1983. (Objectives 2, 3, 7)
   Told in first person, this fantasy unfolds to a startling conclusion as Dawn discovers the mystery of her mother.
Bodecker, N. M. *The Mushroom Center Disaster.* Illustrated by Erik Blegvad. Atheneum, 1975. op. (Objectives 1, 2, 3, 4)
   When the Mushroom Center is destroyed by the careless tossing of picnic trash, Beetle devises a plan to make use of the rubbish.
Calhoun, Mary. *Cross-Country Cat.* Illustrated by Erick Ingraham. William Morrow, 1979. (Objectives 1, 2, 5)
   Henry the cat has to ski his way home when he is accidentally left behind in the mountain cabin.
Daugherty, James. *Andy and the Lion.* Viking, 1938. (Objectives 1, 4)
   Andy reads a book about lions and has an imaginary adventure as a result.
Duvoisin, Roger. *Petunia.* Alfred A. Knopf, 1950. (Objectives 1, 4)
   Petunia, the silly goose, discovers that carrying a book around does not in itself make her wise.
Ehrlich, Amy. *Leo, Zack, and Emmie.* Illustrated by Stephen Kellogg. Dial, 1981. (Objectives 2, 3, 4)
   The new girl in school disrupts the friendship of Leo and Zack.
Gardiner, John Reynolds. *Stone Fox.* Illustrated by Marcia Sewall. Thomas Y. Crowell, 1980. (Objectives 2, 4, 6)
   Little Willy enters a dog sled race to earn the money to pay his grandfather's back taxes.
Greenwald, Sheila. *Rosy Cole's Great American Guilt Club.* Atlantic Monthly, 1985. (Objective 4)
   Rosy tries to make her schoolmates feel guilty so they will give her the clothes she feels are important.
Kipling, Rudyard. *The Elephant's Child.* Illustrated by Lorinda Bryan Cauley. Harcourt Brace Jovanovich, 1983. (Objective 1)
   Humorous rhythmic prose records the tale of the elephant child's curiosity that results in long trunks for all elephants.

Lobel, Arnold. *Fables.* Harper & Row, 1980. (Objectives 1, 2, 3, 4)
   Twenty one-page illustrated original fables about a variety of animals.
McCloskey, Robert. *Lentil.* Viking, 1940. (Objectives 2, 3, 4)
   Lentil's harmonica playing saves the day when Colonel Carter comes back to town.
Miles, Miska. *Annie and the Old One.* Illustrated by Peter Parnall. Little, Brown, 1971. (Objective 4)
   Annie tries to stop the completion of her mother's weaving because Grandmother says she will die when the rug is taken from the loom.
Sharmat, Marjorie Weinman. *Nate the Great Goes Down in the Dumps.* Illustrated by Marc Simont. Coward-McCann, 1989. (Objectives 2, 7)
   Rosamond asks Nate to solve the mystery of her missing money box.
Winthrop, Elizabeth. *Katherine's Doll.* Illustrated by Marylin Hefner. E. P. Dutton, 1983. (Objective 3)
   Molly and Katherine's friendship is tested when one of them receives a beautiful doll.

GROUP INTRODUCTORY ACTIVITY:

Preparing for the Activity: Locate Arnold Lobel's *Fables* and familiarize yourself with the stories. Also review the meanings of climax, rising action, theme, and conflict in the glossary of this book. Using butcher paper, make a chart with the words *Title, Rising action, Conflict, Climax,* and *Theme* across the top as column headings.

Focus: Review, with the students, the idea of problems and solutions in stories. Be certain that all students can identify those terms. Tell them that you will read a fable that has a problem and a lesson.

Objective: To satisfy the objectives of identifying rising action, climax, conflict, and expressing the theme, tell the students that fables are short stories with morals, or lessons. Ask the students to listen for the problem in the story and for a lesson. Tell them that you will have new words for them to learn at the end of the story.

Guided Activity: Read "The Ducks and the Fox" in Lobel's *Fables.* Ask the students to describe the problem between the characters. When they identify it, tell them that this is a conflict—when characters want different things. Sometimes a conflict can mean danger, as in this story. On the chart, write "Ducks and Fox" under the title. Write the conflict in the students' words under that column. Ask for the moment when the ducks make an important discovery. When the students identify the final confrontation, tell them that this is the climax of the story—when the conflicts between characters make one character decide or discover something that solves the conflict. Write the climax in the students' words on the chart.

Once the conflict and climax have been identified, ask for events in the story that led the ducks to their fight with the fox. Write any three of the events they name under *Rising action* on the chart. Explain that rising action is the series of details in the story explaining the conflict or problem that bring the characters to the climax of the story.

When finished with that discussion, read the moral. Explain that every fable has a moral—that is, it teaches a lesson. Ask if the children agree with the moral. Perhaps they have another moral or they could restate Lobel's. Tell the students that the sentence moral of a fable is sometimes called the "theme" of the story, because it is what the story is about. Most stories do not give the statement of theme, and the readers must discover it by thinking about the whole story. Write the students' moral under the heading *Theme.*

Extending Activity: Make a copy of the morals of Lobel's *Fables* and cut them apart so that each student can have a different moral. Ask the students to write and illustrate a fable of their own to match the moral. Invite the students to work with a partner if they wish. Share the class fables. Discuss the elements of climax, conflict, and rising action if appropriate. Have the students read Lobel's fables with the same morals. Collect and bind the students' written fables for a classroom book.

With the complexity of the concepts introduced in this unit, the students will need more guided practice before they master the ideas. As time permits, use others of the fables to reinforce the ideas. Use the chart, and add the students' ideas to it. "The Frog and the End of the Rainbow" and "Pelican and Crane" are two fables that can be used well with this same procedure.

FOLLOW-UP ACTIVITIES FOR TEACHER AND STUDENTS TO SHARE:

1. Before reading Olaf Baker's *Where the Buffaloes Begin,* explain to the students that often authors and illustrators give clues of what is going to happen in the story so that the reader will not be so surprised that the story seems unbelievable. It also can be used to make the reader want to continue the story. This is done through words, illustrations, and, sometimes, chapter titles, and is called foreshadowing. Tell the class that there is foreshadowing in this story so they should listen to the text and watch the illustrations carefully. After reading the story, ask the children if there was an early clue that the Assiniboins were going to Little

Wolf's village. After the children recall that Little Wolf thought he saw something, go back and read the passage about the "dim spot on the yellowish gray of the prairie," and the following page to show that Baker did foreshadow the coming crisis. What was the theme of the story? What events in the story made the class arrive at that theme?

2. Introduce Molly Bang's *Dawn*. Tell the class that there is a mystery and a surprise in the story and they should watch for clues in the words and illustrations. After reading the story, let the children talk about the conflict. Ask the class what discovery by Dawn's father is the climax of the story. Discuss any clues the class saw or heard that hinted how the story would end.

3. Give a brief book talk that describes the setting of N. M. Bodecker's *The Mushroom Center Disaster*. Suggest to the children that those who wish to do so read the book and do one of the individual activities you will provide for them. Tell the class that when as many as wish to do so have finished the book and completed an activity, you will call the group together to discuss the book.

    Let the small group discuss the rising action, conflict, climax, and theme. Then ask the students to relate the story to life today. What problems do the tossing out of litter cause? Suppose someone from outer space threw UFR (Unidentified Flying Rubbish) on the school's neighborhood. What problems could be caused? How would the neighborhood people react? Would they take care of the problem themselves or expect government help? Imagine an object that could be thrown out and think of a way a creative child in the community could suggest it be used.

4. Read Mary Calhoun's *Cross-Country Cat* to the class. Then have the class identify the events that provide the rising action in the story. List their responses on the board. What was the climax?

    Suggest that the class suppose the cat was left after the family's summer visit to the cabin. Have the class review the list of events that provided the rising action for Calhoun's story. Have the class think of a set of events for the summer cat that could lead to a similar climax. Suggest that members of the class who wish to do so illustrate the scenes in the summer story and write a brief text describing the action. Put the scenes together. The teacher may provide needed text links to make a story of the summer cat.

5. Before reading James Daugherty's *Andy and the Lion*, tell the class that Daugherty had hoped the book would be published with no words. His editor did not agree and helped him write the text. Tell the students that you are going to cover the words and see if they can use only the pictures to describe the rising action that leads to the climax. After the students try to tell the story, read the text as you show them the illustrations again. See if they were able to get an accurate idea of the rising action

when using the pictures only. What is the theme of the story? What events caused them to make their decisions?

Ask the students to go home and tell Daugherty's story to their parents or an adult. See if it reminds them of any other story they have heard. Have the students ask the adults to tell them their stories. Give the students time to share any stories the adults tell. What are the similarities in events? Are the themes similar?

6. Read Roger Duvoisin's *Petunia* to the class. What is the theme of the story? Have the students recall the rising action and the lines of the characters in each scene. Let students act out the story.

7. Before reading "A New Girl" from Amy Ehrlich's *Leo, Zack, and Emmie,* ask the class if anyone has ever lost a friend because someone new moved into the neighborhood. If so, how did it make them feel? Read the story "A New Girl" to the class. What is the conflict in the story? What is the climax? What is a theme for this first story?

Suggest that each member of the class who wishes to do so read one of the other stories in the book. Ask them to write down the conflict, climax, and theme to share with the class. Are the themes of the other stories similar to the theme found in "A New Girl"?

8. Read to the class Rudyard Kipling's *The Elephant's Child* illustrated by Lorinda Cauley. Beforehand urge them to enjoy the humorous words as well as to keep in mind the rising action and climax of the story. After reading the story, let the students recall the events that provide the rising action in the story. The class can pantomime those scenes as the teacher reads each one. Those not acting in the scenes can participate as a chorus by saying "And still he was full of 'satiable curtiosity'" and "the great grey-green greasy Limpopo River all set about by fever-trees" as needed in the story.

9. Read Robert McCloskey's *Lentil* to the class. Discuss the conflicts in the story. How is each resolved? What is the climax of the story? What is the theme? Was the rising action of the band being unable to play because Mr. Sneep sucked a lemon realistic? Would it have been more realistic if Mr. Sneep had convinced each member of the band to suck a lemon so they could play better? Give a volunteer a slice of lemon and see if he or she can play a wind instrument. If not, then every band member's sucking a lemon would have been more realistic than McCloskey's scene. If someone can play the harmonica, let the class sing "Comin' 'round the mountain when she comes."

10. Read Elizabeth Winthrop's *Katherine's Doll* to the class. Discuss Katherine's and Molly's feelings after Katherine gets her doll. Identify words and pictures that show the conflict. How did they resolve the conflict? Does that seem logical? Will they have

other conflicts? Ask the students to bring a favorite doll, toy, or stuffed animal and tell the class what makes it special.

FOLLOW-UP ACTIVITIES FOR INDIVIDUALS OR SMALL GROUPS:

1. Read John Gardiner's *Stone Fox.* Write the theme of the story and explain what made you decide on that theme.
2. Read John Gardiner's *Stone Fox.* Would you have chosen that climax? Write another climax Gardiner might have used.
3. Read John Gardiner's *Stone Fox.* Write a paragraph about what would happen next if the story were one chapter longer.
4. Read Sheila Greenwald's *Rosy Cole's Great American Guilt Club.* Write a theme for the story. What events in the story made you decide on that theme?
5. Read Miska Miles' *Annie and the Old One.* Copy the words of grandmother that are Miles' theme of the story. Now state that theme in your own words.
6. Read Marjorie Sharmat's *Nate the Great Goes Down in the Dumps.* Write down the climax. List any clues you found that foreshadowed how the mystery would be solved.

Vocabulary

STUDENT OBJECTIVES:

1. Identify descriptive words used to describe the setting of a story.
2. Select and create sight and sound imagery words.
3. Select a sentence describing an object or action and rewrite, using figurative language.
4. Select a sentence with figurative language and rewrite as children would probably have said it.
5. Identify colloquial language in a story.
6. Create degrees of comparison in adjectives.
7. Determine the meaning of words.

RECOMMENDED READING:

Baskin, Hosea, Tobias, and Lisa. *Hosie's Alphabet.* Illustrated by Leonard Baskin. Viking, 1972, op. (Objective 7)
Picturesque phrases and striking illustrations combine to make an imaginative, thought-provoking whole.

Berger, Barbara. *Grandfather Twilight.* Philomel, 1984. (Objective 2)
As evening comes, Grandfather Twilight takes a pearl to the woods to bring light to the night.

Birdseye, Tom. *Airmail to the Moon.* Illustrated by Stephen Gammell. Holiday House, 1988. (Objective 5)
Ora Mae threatens to send the thief that stole her tooth "airmail to the moon."

Caudill, Rebecca. *A Pocketful of Cricket.* Illustrated by Evaline Ness. Holt, Rinehart and Winston, 1964. (Objectives 2, 3)
Jay makes friends with a cricket and takes it to school with him.

Fleischman, Sid. *The Scarebird.* Illustrated by Peter Sis. Greenwillow, 1988. (Objectives 2, 4, 5)
A lonely farmer befriends a young man to the benefit of both.

Kraus, Ruth. *A Hole Is to Dig.* Illustrated by Maurice Sendak. Harper & Row, 1952. (Objective 7)
Nursery school children give definitions for familiar objects.

McMillan, Bruce. *Super Super Superwords.* Lothrop, Lee & Shepard, 1989. (Objective 6)
Photographs and identifying words demonstrate the three degrees of comparison in adjectives.

Martin, Bill, Jr., and John Archambault. *Listen to the Rain.* Illustrated by James Endicott. Henry Holt, 1988. (Objective 2)
Rhythmic text describes the changing sounds of the rain.

Minarik, Else Holmelund. *Percy and the Five Houses.* Illustrated by James Stevenson. Greenwillow, 1989. (Objective 3)
Percy, the beaver, finds that no "House of the Month" is a satisfactory home for him.

Nixon, Joan Lowery. *Beats Me, Claude.* Illustrated by Tracey Campbell Pearson. Viking, 1986. (Objective 5)
Colloquial language adds to the humor in this tale of Shirley's attempts to make an apple pie.

Radin, Ruth Yaffe. *High in the Mountains.* Illustrated by Ed Young. Macmillan, 1989. (Objectives 1, 2, 3)
Figurative language and striking illustrations reveal a young person's enjoyment of the high mountains near Grandpa's house.

Ryder, Joanne. *Step into the Night.* Illustrated by Dennis Nolan. Four Winds, 1988. (Objective 2)
Poetic text and luminous illustrations picture a girl's thoughts about the tiny animals who inhabit the night.

Stolz, Mary. *Storm in the Night.* Illustrated by Pat Cummings. Harper
& Row, 1988. (Objective 2)
Suspense is heightened by the figurative language used to tell of a
grandfather's fear of storms when he was a boy.

Thiele, Colin. *Farmer Schulz's Ducks.* Illustrated by Mary Milton.
Harper & Row, 1988. (Objectives 1, 2, 4)
Figurative language enlivens the story of how the ducks on an
Australian farm escape death from dangerous traffic.

Wildsmith, Brian. *Wild Animals.* Oxford University, 1976, paper.
(Objective 7)
Groups of different animals are illustrated with the text identify-
ing the label denoting each group.

Zolotow, Charlotte. *Say It!* Illustrated by James Stevenson.
Greenwillow, 1980. (Objective 2)
A little girl and her mother enjoy the sights and sounds as they
walk through the woods on an autumn day.

GROUP INTRODUCTORY ACTIVITY:

Preparing for the Activity: Locate Joanne Ryder's *Step into the Night.*
Have several three-dimensional geometric shapes on hand to show the
class. For the extending activity, have ready butcher paper for a
mural or bulletin board.

Focus: Begin by explaining to the students that authors sometimes try
to make their words so exact that readers can almost see pictures in
their minds or hear the sounds described in stories. Show the student
several blocks or geometric shapes. Ask what kinds of words could be
used to describe these objects—lead the students to words describing
shape, size, and color. Next, ask them to describe the sounds of a
wind, a rainstorm, and children playing a game. Lead them to words
describing volume, pitch, and tone.

Objective: To satisfy the objective of selecting sight imagery and
sound imagery in descriptive passages, tell the children that the book
you will share includes many words that make sight and sound
pictures. They will need to listen for words that, with their imagination, make sight or sound images.

Guided Activity: Read Ryder's *Step into the Night.* Give time for the
students to enjoy both the words and pictures. Point out that the
story is told from different points of view—the girl's and each of the
animal's.
When finished, ask the students if they remember any sight
words or sound words from the story that made pictures in their
imagination. Find the pages and reread the phrases. Introduce the

terms *sight image* and *sound image*. Point out, if the students do not, such terms as "soft berries, eat-me-red," "a chunk of the moon," "cries bounce off," "night is full of voices," "deep, rough voice."

Extending Activity: As a follow-up, begin a class collection of sight and sound images. On a mural or a bulletin board write two or three phrases from this book. Include author and title. Suggest to the students that they search the books they read for sight and sound images and invite them to add to the imagery list, always including the author and title. As you read other books to the class, suggest that the students look for more images. Urge them to use those images in conversation when appropriate.

FOLLOW-UP ACTIVITIES FOR TEACHER AND STUDENTS TO SHARE:

1. Before reading the Baskins' *Hosie's Alphabet,* tell the children they will hear a number of new words and they will be asked later to try and figure out the meaning. When finished, return to L. Explain how locusts in groups will eat everything in their path. Ask the class to think what omnivorous might mean. Turn to Z. Tell the children that zebras, like cows, chew and chew their food. Have them guess the meaning of "ruminating." Point out other words and also ask the class to notice phrases that begin with the same sounds.

2. Before reading Barbara Berger's *Grandfather Twilight,* tell the class that there are textless pages where they should observe the illustrations and think of sight or sound words to tell the story. Read the book to the class, having the children merely look at the illustrations on the textless pages without attempting to fill in words.

   Now reread the story. Have children notice the sound imagery on the pages preceding the textless pages. Have the class create figurative text for the pages with illustrations only. Suggest they notice the animals and the pictures of Grandfather Twilight to get ideas.

3. Talk about colloquial language. Give children examples of old sayings used locally. Ask the class to listen for *colloquial expressions* as you read Tom Birdseye's *Airmail to the Moon.* After reading the story, see how many of Ora Mae's expressions they can recall. Reread the text and let them note other expressions they have forgotten. Have students act out the story; urge the actors to use the colloquial language of the story.

4. Before reading Rebecca Caudill's *A Pocketful of Cricket,* tell the children that the book has many sight and sound words that will help them picture the farm where Jay lives. As you read the first few pages, stop to note briefly the figurative language they have

heard such as "The great pinkish crown nodded on tall stalks" and "The smell tingled in his nose like the smell of the first frost." Continue reading, asking the children to remember descriptive phrases until the story is over. Then discuss the words they remember. Were they helped in picturing the scene by the words used?

List the items the children recall that Jay thought of bringing to "Show and Tell." Ask the children to describe each, making a word picture more complete than that given by Caudill.

5. Before reading Sid Fleischman's *The Scarebird,* urge the class to listen for the colloquial language characteristic of the farm community. After reading the story let the class recall phrases they have heard such as "cold creeps," "sunshine on stilts," "sun rising like a blow torch." Have them note whether those recalled were sight or sound imagery words. Start a list of the words on butcher paper. What would the students have said instead of the colloquial language? Which is more colorful? Suggest that members of the class reread the story and add to the colloquial word list. Ask them to suggest how they would have said each phrase added.

   Have the class ask their grandparents or older adults if they can recall expressions not in common use now. Have them report these expressions to the class.

6. Before reading Ruth Kraus' *A Hole Is to Dig,* tell the children that the definitions in this book were given by nursery school children. Read the book to the class.

   Before reading the book again, suggest to the children that they make up more appropriate definitions. Give them a pattern for the meanings they create; for example, "mashed potatoes are vegetables that are soft and easy to eat," or "A face is a part of the body that contains eyes, nose, and mouth." Thus, the pattern is to give the whole or group to which the word belongs and then describe it. Let the children redo each of the definitions in the book.

   Suggest that as the children go home at the end of the day, they observe one object and write a definition. Bring the definition to school and share, with the class discussing whether each follows the pattern. Kraus' book could be an introduction to a dictionary unit.

7. Read to the class Bruce McMillan's choice of adjective comparisons in *Super Super Superwords.* Name the three degrees of comparison and ask the class to volunteer other adjectives they can compare. Urge them to think of adjectives that contrast to those given by McMillan. Divide the class in half and play a game where one side thinks of a positive term and the other side thinks of the comparative and superlative.

8. Before reading to the class Bill Martin and John Archambault's *Listen to the Rain,* have the class suggest words identifying the sounds of rain. List their responses on the board. Tell them to listen carefully because afterwards you will ask them to recall the sounds Martin suggests. As they recall the sounds after the book is read, make a new list on the board. Talk about which list creates the most word pictures in their minds.

   Suppose Martin and Archambault wrote a book *Listen to the Wind.* Urge the class to suggest the sounds of wind they might include.

9. Before reading Else Holmelund Minarik's *Percy and the Five Houses,* explain to the class that the illustrations are used to give sight imagery to the book instead of the simple text. Suggest that they examine the illustrations carefully as you read so that sight imagery descriptions can be created for the "Houses of the Month." After reading the story, go back to look at each of the five houses of the month. Urge the children to use figurative language to describe each house. Record their words on the blackboard as they make suggestions.

10. Before reading Joan Nixon's *Beats Me, Claude,* have the children discuss the title. What is the meaning of the expression "Beats Me"? Tell the class that there are many expressions in the story that were used most by rural people in earlier times. Have them listen for such words as "afore" and "hankerin." Keep a record of those the students notice so that after the story is read, they can discuss the meaning of each. At first, if they have difficulty hearing the colloquial language, read some sentences again. Talk about the meaning of the words on the list after the story is completed. Refer to the text if needed.

11. Before reading Ruth Radin's *High in the Mountains* to the class, urge them to listen for the sight and sound imagery words that show the child's sense of wonder at the mountain setting. After reading the book, let students recall the expressions they remember. Then read the book again so they will not miss any of the images such as the shadow "like a giant lying down" and the road that "wraps like elastic around each shape." On the pages where there are no special descriptive phrases about their car trip and overnight camping, urge the class to study Young's illustrations and create sight image text.

   If any of the class has made a trip to the mountains and taken pictures, urge them to bring the photographs to place on the bulletin board. Let children caption them with favorite appropriate phrases from Radin's book.

12. Read Mary Stolz's *Storm in the Night* aloud to the class. Then read the first page again, asking the children to listen for words telling what the thunder was like, what the lightning did, the sound of the rain, and the color of the flames. Make two lists on the board. Label one *Seeing words* and the other *Hearing words.*

Talk about those words listed thus far. Let the children suggest words they might have used. Did Stolz's words create a more exciting picture of the storm?

Continue to read, letting children point out figurative language. Continue the list on the blackboard in the appropriate column. Help children note the exciting verbs used in the lines: "just then a bolt of lightning cracked into the big beech tree! It ripped off a mighty bough which crashed to the ground." What words would the children have used? Were Stolz's choices better?

When the second reading is completed, review the blackboard lists. Were there more sight images or sound images? Why?

13. Before reading Colin Thiele's *Farmer Schulz's Ducks,* tell the class that the book was written by an Australian author. Show them Australia and the United States on the globe. Tell them the book is full of descriptive words that will help them picture the setting of an Australian farm. Ask them to listen carefully so they can recall some of the descriptive words when the story is over. After reading the story, ask the children to recall any sight or sound imagery that will help them picture the scene. Talk about how they might have said those descriptive phrases.

    Now read the first eight pages again. Ask the children to hold up their hands as soon as they hear some sight or sound imagery words that are memorable. Either start a sight and a sound imagery list on butcher paper or the blackboard or continue one already begun with another book. As a follow-up, urge the children to read the story again and add to the list.

14. Before reading Brian Wildsmith's *Wild Animals,* have the class try to think of words meaning a group of a specific type of animal, such as a flock of birds or a school of fish. Read the introduction to the book ahead of time to prepare yourself for this discussion.

    Read the book, giving the students time to examine the illustrations as you read the identifying group term. Discuss the meaning of the word and give the class time to think about why a "nursery" of raccoons, an "ambush" of tigers, and a "shrewdness" of apes, etc., are appropriate.

    When the book is finished, have the class think of group terms for domesticated animals. Suggest they discuss these words with parents or adults to add new ones or reinforce their ideas. Have the class select an animal group to illustrate and label with the correct group term. Make an "Animal Groups" bulletin board.

15. Introduce Charlotte Zolotow's *Say It!* by telling the children to listen for words that make pictures in their minds. After reading the book, ask if anyone remembers color words, shape words, or action words. Refer to the book again as needed.

Have the class take a brief walk and notice the sights and sounds. Come back and let the class create sentences full of sight/sound imagery to describe what they saw and heard on the walk. Record their responses.

FOLLOW-UP ACTIVITIES FOR INDIVIDUALS OR SMALL GROUPS:

1. Reread Rebecca Caudill's *A Pocketful of Cricket*. Divide the story into three logical chapters and write the name of each one. Share your chapter titles with the teacher.
2. Reread *Listen to the Rain* by Bill Martin and John Archambault. Using the title "Listen to the Hail," write two sound image descriptions to fit that title. Read them to the teacher or class.
3. Reread Else Minarik's *Percy and the Five Houses*. Think of a different "House of the Month." Create or illustrate it and write a descriptive paragraph to give a word image of its appearance. Tell why Percy did not find it to be satisfactory for him.
4. Reread Joan Nixon's *Beats Me, Claude*. Write a name for each of the three chapters, using the language Shirley or Claude may have used. Share with the class.
5. Reread Charlotte Zolotow's *Say It!* After your next ride in the car or walk to a friend's house, write a paragraph. Use sight imagery words to describe what you saw. Share your paragraph with the class.

Discovering Information Books

STUDENT OBJECTIVES:

1. Follow directions and create a product from a how-to-do-it book.
2. Share facts about caring for a pet you have or would like to have.
3. Explore possible hobbies.
4. Find facts about a subject of interest to share with classmates.
5. Identify some information books in the Dewey classification of Pure Sciences (500s), Technology (600s), The Arts (700s), and Geography and History (900s).

RECOMMENDED READING:

Aliki. *Dinosaur Bones.* Thomas Y. Crowell, 1988. (Objectives 4, 5)
Introduces the way scientists study fossil remains to gain information about dinosaurs and how they lived.

Blocksma, Mary and Dewey. *Action Contraptions.* Illustrated by Sandra Hulst. Prentice-Hall, 1987. (Objectives 1, 5)
Simple instructions for making movable toys from household and inexpensive items.

Branley, Franklyn. *Tornado Alert.* Illustrated by Giulio Maestro. Thomas Y. Crowell, 1988. (Objectives 4, 5)
Describes how tornadoes form, when and where they most frequently threaten, and how to remain safe.

de Paola, Tomie. *The Popcorn Book.* Holiday House, 1978. (Objectives 4, 5)
While one child makes popcorn, the other child reads facts about it.

Gans, Roma. *Rock Collecting.* Illustrated by Holly Keeler. Thomas Y. Crowell, 1984. (Objectives 3, 4, 5)
Describes how to recognize igneous, sedimentary, and metamorphic rocks, and how to begin a rock collection.

Gibbons, Gail. *Sunken Treasure.* Thomas Y. Crowell, 1988. (Objectives 4, 5)
Describes the search to recover the treasure from the Spanish ship, the *Atoka*, lost in a hurricane off Florida in 1622.

Irvine, Joan. *How to Make Pop-Ups.* Illustrated by Barbara Reid. William Morrow, 1987. (Objectives 1, 5)
Gives step-by-step directions for making pop-up books and cards.

Kuklin, Susan. *Taking My Dog to the Vet.* Bradbury, 1988. (Objectives 2, 4, 5)
A veterinarian examines a child's dog and discusses possible health problems that the dog might have at a future time.

Robbins, Ken. *At the Ballpark.* Viking, 1988. (Objectives 4, 5)
Photographs enhance the simple text describing the fun of a baseball game.

Simon, Seymour. *Soap Bubble Magic.* Illustrated by Stella Ormai. Lothrop, Lee & Shepard, 1985. (Objectives 1, 4, 5)
Experiments demonstrate the characteristics of soap bubbles.

Simon, Seymour. *Storms.* William Morrow, 1989. (Objective 4)
Concise text and dramatic photography identify types of violent storms.

Yoshida, Toshi. *Young Lions.* Philomel, 1989. (Objective 4)
Three lion cubs hunt unsuccessfully but see many other animals on the African plain.

GROUP INTRODUCTORY ACTIVITY:

Preparing for the Activity: Locate *Soap Bubble Magic* by Seymour Simon. For the demonstrations, set up a table at the front of the area with all the supplies and materials ready for the students: liquid detergent, a bar of soap, bowls and glasses, a supply of water, loops for blowing bubbles, needles, pepper, and foil for a boat. Protect the table top and floor.

Begin a mural or bulletin board to be used during this unit to collect the titles and authors of nonfiction books under their proper Dewey Decimal classifications. Divide the mural or bulletin board into spaces for books in the 500s, 600s, 700s, and 900s. Leave room for titles and authors to be written.

Focus: Before reading the book to the class, ask the students to tell you everything they know about soap and bubbles. How do bubbles keep their shape? Why are they round? Why can you see colors and your reflection in bubbles? After the students have explored their knowledge, ask them how they could discover more about bubbles if they wanted to. Where would they look for more information?

Objective: To satisfy the objectives of identifying the Dewey Classification of information books, following directions, and finding facts about a subject of interest, tell the students that you have a book that will answer some of the questions you asked about bubbles. Tell them that they will learn some new information about soap, and they will have a chance to participate in experiments using soap and water. Suggest that you want everyone to remember five new facts about soap and bubbles from the book.

Guided Activity: Read Seymour Simon's *Soap Bubble Magic.* When the book directs the reader to conduct an experiment, ask for two volunteers to follow the directions as you read them. The rest of the class should listen and decide if the volunteers are following the directions correctly. Discuss the results of each activity and continue reading. For each activity call on different students. Allow as many as possible to participate in the activities. Let the students discuss what they observe and decide if there is significance to the observations.

Ask the students to tell you what new information they learned from this book. Explain to the students that this is an information book and is catalogued in the 700s of the Dewey Classification. This means that it is a book that is classified in "The Arts." Ask them if they can tell you why they think this would be an arts book. Ask for other kinds of books that would be considered arts books. At this time, show the students the mural or bulletin board, and tell them that during this unit, the class will keep track of the information books and their classification numbers. Write the author and title of this book under 700s on the mural. Tell the students that as the group reads information books, or as they read them individually, they may add to the author/title/classification list.

Extending Activity: Since every student did not have the opportunity to conduct all the experiments in the book, set up an area in the room where students may go to reread the book and complete the activities on their own. Have the students write a paragraph describing their activity and their findings.

Ask volunteers to research soap bubbles in the library and report to the class on any additional information. Have the students decide on possible sources of information on the topic and consult the media specialist.

FOLLOW-UP ACTIVITIES FOR TEACHER AND STUDENTS TO SHARE:

1. Introduce Aliki's *Dinosaur Bones* by asking the children if any of them have ever visited a museum. If so, what did they see there? In this book the child visits a natural history museum and sees dinosaur bones. The book describes how scientists studied fossils to put together information about specific dinosaurs and how they lived. Call attention to the classification of 567.9 in the Pure Sciences category. Other fact books about dinosaurs will have that number also.

    Ask the class to listen for facts about the fossil searches. Read the book and let the children recall how information was gathered. What does the word "dinosaur" mean?

    Show the class the list of the dinosaurs pictured, the meaning of each word, and then locate on the globe where each kind of dinosaur originally lived. Ask those students who are interested in dinosaurs to select a specific dinosaur and seek facts about it in the library to share with the class. Perhaps the school librarian can use interlibrary loan to locate dinosaur books because many in the class will probably be interested. If a natural history museum that displays dinosaur bones is nearby, you may wish to plan a field trip to extend information found in books.

2. Introduce Franklyn Branley's *Tornado Alert* by asking the class to name kinds of storms that people fear. Tell the class that this book describes tornadoes. Ask them to note where tornadoes are most likely a threat, how people are warned, and what safety measures they can follow. Call attention to the 551.5 classification number. This is in the Pure Sciences category, and other fact books on weather will be found under this number in the library.

    Read the book to the class. Let the children discuss the facts presented. Are the tornado rules listed on the last page useful for

other storms as well? Show the class Seymour Simon's *Storms.*
Ask those in the class who are interested to read this book, do a
suggested individual activity, and share it with the class. After
the students have shared storm information, ask a weatherman
from the nearest TV studio to come to the class and talk about
weather safety.

3. Introduce Tomie de Paola's *The Popcorn Book* by asking the
class what facts they know about popcorn. Tell the class that
they will learn many facts as the children in the book prepare to
eat popcorn. Notice that the book is catalogued 641.6. This is
Foods, a part of the Technology classification.

   After reading the book to the class, let them recall the facts
about popcorn that they learned. Read the recipe for Friday
Night Popcorn. Is that the way they make popcorn at home?
How is popcorn usually made now? Of course, the children
should get to eat popcorn as they discuss the book.

   Now suppose the boys wanted to make chocolate fudge.
What questions might be asked to send one boy to the encyclo-
pedia? List the questions the children suggest on the blackboard.
Ask a small committee to go to the library and try to find the
answers. Perhaps if they also find other information they can
write and illustrate a simple book patterned after de Paola's.
They will want to include an easy-to-make fudge recipe at the
end of the book.

4. Introduce Roma Gans' *Rock Collecting* by asking if anyone in
the class has a collecting hobby. After the children tell what they
collect, ask if anyone has read books about their type of collection. Why would that be a good idea? Show the children the title
and the classification number on the book. Ask: Will all books
about any type of collection be in that number? Why not? After
children establish that only books about rock collecting have
that number, tell them that as you read they are to listen for
facts about rocks as well as ways to organize rocks they collect.

   After the book is read, let students discuss facts about the
three types of rocks and hints for beginning rock collectors. Ask
if anyone has an organized rock collection he or she would like
to share with the class. The class may want to find other books
about rocks and start a class rock collection, labeling them in
the categories of igneous, sedimentary, or metamorphic.

   Suggest that children with other types of collections may
want to find a book in the school or public library about the
objects they collect. They may want to bring part of their
collection to share with the class as well as facts found in the
books they read. Remind them to tell the class the classification
number under which books on that hobby are found and to add
their book to the class list of information books read.

5. Introduce Gail Gibbon's *Sunken Treasure* by asking the class if
they know why the book has this name. After they respond, ask

if anyone knows the name of any famous ships that have sunk. Tell the class that this book is the factual account of the attempt to salvage the treasure on the *Atoka*, a Spanish ship sunk off Florida in 1622. The book is found in the library under 910.4 for Buried Treasure, part of the Geography and History section.

Ask the children to listen as the book is read for problems in locating the ship, how records were kept of the things found, and how items were cared for. What proof was there that the ship was really the *Atoka*?

After discussing the book, tell the class that in the back of the book are descriptions of four other ships that were lost and have now been salvaged. Someone may want to read that information, then go to the library and find out more about the sinking and the locating of the *Titanic*, one of the ships briefly described, so they can share with the class.

6. Introduce Joan Irvine's *How to Make Pop-Ups* by asking if the children have ever followed directions and made paper objects. Tell them that this book is classified in 736, Paper Cutting and Folding, in The Arts section of the library. Read aloud the directions for making window cards, pages 58–61. Read again and demonstrate, letting the children follow directions and make a window card for a parent or someone special.

Suggest that you will leave the book on the library table. Perhaps individual class members or small groups may want to read the directions and make something else from paper to share with the class.

Show the class Mary and Dewey Blocksma's *Action Contraptions*. Show them that it is also classified in The Arts. Suggest some may want to take the book home, follow directions, and make a toy to show the class.

7. Introduce Susan Kuklin's *Taking My Dog to the Vet* by asking: How many of you have taken pets to the vet? Why? What problems did you or your pet have? Tell them to listen for the child's and dog's experiences in order to compare with their own.

Read the book. Let the children discuss the way the veterinarian treated the child and the dog. Tell the class the Dewey classification is 636.7. Why would the pet books be in the Technology section? If they have no ideas, tell them the 600 section is also called Applied Science. Ask the class: Can the care of a pet be called a hobby? What is a hobby?

Ask the children to find a book in the library about a pet they have or would like to have. After they read the book, they should list ten facts they would like to share with the class. Ask them to draw a picture of their dream pets or bring a photograph of their own pets. Have a pet sharing hour in which each child shares the picture and one fact that would be interesting to others. If possible, ask a veterinarian to visit the class and talk about pet care.

8. Introduce Ken Robbins' *At the Ballpark* by asking if anyone in the class has ever attended a professional baseball game, either big league or farm club. Tell the class that in this book photographs try to capture the excitement of the game. Ask them to watch for the teams that are playing and what makes it fun for the spectators. Note that baseball is classified as 796.357, and it is in The Arts section of the library.

   After reading the book to the class, place a title on the board "I Enjoyed the Baseball Game Because." Ask the children to suggest reasons why they would enjoy being at the game. What major league teams were pictured? Suggest that those who are interested make little pennants giving major league team names and place them at the appropriate sites on a large map of the United States. If the map shows a bit of Canada, they can locate the two Canadian teams also.

9. Introduce Toshi Yoshida's *Young Lions* by locating Africa's Mount Kilimanjaro on the world map. Tell the class that this is the setting for the book. Point out that Yoshida used colored pencil to draw the illustrations. He introduced brief facts about many animals that the young lions see. Ask the class to listen carefully and see what animals and facts they can remember.

   Read the book. Then show the class the end papers. See how many animals they can identify and any facts they can remember about the animals. Refer to the text as needed.

FOLLOW-UP ACTIVITIES FOR INDIVIDUALS OR SMALL GROUPS:

1. Read Seymour Simon's *Storms*. Now reread the part about thunderstorms, lightning, hailstorms, downdrafts, and windshear, *or* hurricanes. List five facts you want to share with the class. Show the photographs that relate to your facts.
2. Read Seymour Simon's *Storms*. Now reread the part about tornadoes. Share with the class any new information not found in Franklyn Branley's *Tornado Alert*.
3. Examine the illustrations in Toshi Yoshida's *Young Lions* after the book is read in class. Select one animal and research more information about it. Make a colored pencil or crayon drawing of the animal and list below five facts about it.

Chapter 3
Fourth Grade/Fifth Grade

At the fourth and fifth grade levels the focus shifts from specific skills and strategies to evaluation of the merit of works in specific literary genres. This chapter helps the teacher introduce literary terminology and use it in analysis and criticism of children's poetry, novels, and information books. Because of the vital need for all citizens to be visually literate, this concept is continued in a unit that concentrates on symbols and subtleties of illustrations as well as observations of nature. The material and objectives will challenge older learners.

Units begin with group activities, which the teacher introduces by reading all or part of a book to the class. The books selected for these activities are highly motivating, and the teacher should stress the enjoyment he or she derives from reading *to* the class.

Individual activities are designed for a range of developmental and academic levels, and should allow a teacher to assure successful experiences for all students. Almost all the books suggested for a unit are introduced by the teacher because his or her enthusiasm will motivate the student to read the work and continue the individual activities.

Communication and creativity are still expected of the students as they interact with the books. Students will write, experimenting with the forms of literature they are reading. Any time a student creates written work, the teacher should use the writing as an opportunity to extend the experiences of all students.

Although the term "readers theater" was not used, the students are asked to create and read scripts utilizing the conversation in a specific chapter of some of the suggested books. This mode of communication is enjoyable and much less time-consuming than creative dramatics. Another method of sharing is utilized at this level—formal book discussion. Book discussion by a small group of students with the teacher as leader provides a natural avenue for using the terms that are inherent in literary criticism.

Two units include activities that can be shared with families at an open house or through a class newspaper. The activities for the classics unit culminate with a party or reception for parents to enjoy the creative efforts of the students. The fantasy unit includes several suggestions to extend the activity by writing a factual newspaper account of the events or characters in a fantasy. These can be collected and combined into a class paper to be duplicated and circulated.

At this level students are expected and encouraged to become independent readers and to share their experiences with literature. Combining these activities with a sustained silent reading time daily and a reading program that values literature will give children the opportunity to become literate students who can read and choose to do so.

Becoming Visually Literate

STUDENT OBJECTIVES:

1. Recognize the meaning of symbols used by artists in picture books.
2. Note visual subtleties inserted by the artist for discriminating readers.
3. Assess the contribution of the illustrator in giving clues to the country or region of origin, mood, and characters.
4. Describe the theme, plot, setting, and characters in a wordless picture book.

RECOMMENDED READING:

Andersen, Hans Christian. *The Little Match Girl.* Illustrated by Rachel Isadora. G. P. Putnam's Sons, 1987. (Objective 3)
Full-page illustrations set the mood of the story of the poor girl out in the cold night and of her brief, bright visions.

Anno, Mitsumasa. *Anno's Aesop.* Orchard, 1989. (Objective 3)
Anno illustrates forty-one Aesop's fables, and "Mr. Fox" tells his version of the story depicted in each illustration.

Anno, Mitsumasa. *Anno's Journey.* Philomel, 1981. (Objective 2)
The textless record of a traveler's journey through northern Europe includes people, art, architecture, and literature.

Anno, Mitsumasa. *Anno's Italy.* Philomel, 1984. (Objective 2)
In a textless picture book, Anno illustrates a trip through Italy, showing the countryside, art, architecture, and literature.

Anno, Mitsumasa. *In Shadowland.* Orchard, 1988. (Objective 3)
Life in Shadowland is upset as the watchman goes to the real world to be with the little match girl.

de Paola, Tomie. *The Hunter and the Animals.* Holiday House, 1981. (Objective 4)
The theme of respect for wildlife is conveyed in this wordless picture book.

Geisert, Arthur. *Pigs from A to Z.* Houghton Mifflin, 1986. (Objective 2)
As seven little pigs build a treehouse, the twenty-six illustrations hide five forms of the letters of the alphabet and the pigs themselves.

Kellogg, Steven. *Pecos Bill.* William Morrow, 1986. (Objective 2)
Illustrations add to the humorous retelling of the life of Pecos Bill from his childhood to his wedding.

Mayer, Marianna. *The Twelve Dancing Princesses.* Illustrated by K. Y. Craft. William Morrow, 1989. (Objective 3)
Peter, the gardener's boy, breaks the evil spell that holds the king's twelve beautiful daughters.

McDermott, Gerald. *Arrow to the Sun.* Viking, 1974. (Objective 1)
In this Pueblo Indian tale a boy seeks his immortal father, the Lord of the Sun, and takes his father's spirit back to earth.

McDermott, Gerald. *The Stonecutter.* Viking, 1975, o.p. Penguin, 1978, paper. (Objective 1)
A Japanese folktale of the poor stonecutter whose wishes for wealth and power were granted but gave no satisfaction.

Rogasky, Barbara. *The Water of Life.* Illustrated by Trina Schart Hyman. Holiday House, 1986. (Objectives 1, 2, 3)
Vivid illustrations show the varied moods of the Grimm fairy tale of the young prince who finally outwits his cruel brothers to save his father's life.

Ward, Lynd. *The Silver Pony.* Houghton Mifflin, 1975. (Objectives 3, 4)
With the help of a winged pony, a lonely farm boy finds a commonality between his life and that of others.

Zelinsky, Paul. *Rumpelstiltskin.* E. P. Dutton, 1986. (Objective 3)
The text of this illustrator's Caldecott Honor book is based on the Grimm brothers' version of the familiar tale.

Zemach, Harve. *Duffy and the Devil.* Illustrated by Margot Zemach. Farrar, Straus & Giroux, 1973, 1986. (Objective 3)
Folk art adds to the humor of this Cornish version of the Rumpelstiltskin tale.

GROUP INTRODUCTORY ACTIVITY:

Preparing for the Activity: Locate Barbara Rogasky's *The Water of Life,* illustrated by Trina Schart Hyman. Also locate other books illustrated by the same artist for the extending activity.

Focus: Remind the class that in a well-illustrated book, there are many clues to the story in the illustrations as well as in the text. The proficient reader must know how to read pictures as well as words. Ask the class if they can think of objects or animals that remind them of different seasons or times of the day. Do the list orally.

Objective: To satisfy the objectives of recognizing symbols used by artists, noting visual subtleties inserted by the artist, and assessing the contribution in giving clues to mood and characters, share Rogasky's *The Water of Life.* Before reading the book, introduce the artist, Trina Schart Hyman. Explain to the class that she enjoys adding details to her illustrations that give depth and understanding to the words of the book. Tell them that you will read the words so that they can read the illustrations. Explain that you will ask them to tell you what details in the pictures and borders kept track of the seasons of the year, about the animals she inserted into the illustrations, and what the animals stand for. Have the students ready to look for characterizations within the illustrations. Tell them that they will have to be extremely observant in order to find all the subtleties and details.

Guided Activity: Read *The Water of Life* to the class, leaving plenty of time for the students to study the illustrations. Tell them that you will reread the story to allow for more observation. When you have gone over the story twice, ask for the students' impressions: What did the illustrations add to the story? How did they help visualize the settings and the seasons? Have the students contrast the characters of the princes, using the illustrations. Ask them to describe how the princes look, how they react to others, and their body language. Refer to the illustrations of the brothers reunited after the youngest one rescues the others and the following one of the war-ravaged country. Return to the beginning of the book, and study the border details, tracing the seasons and years. Identify the birds and animals. You may have to explain why ravens are appropriate for the pictures of death and destruction, but the students should be able to tell why the owl appears as the youngest prince is escaping the castle at midnight. Study the illustrations of the princess. How is she different from other fairy-tale princesses? With what prized possessions does she choose to surround herself? What does that tell about her? Describe the people she works with. Show the illustrations of the troll seeming to watch over the youngest prince. Ask: Why would he be doing this?

Study the final illustrations. How do the illustrations carry the story along to its conclusion?

Extending Activity: Have enough copies of other books Hyman has illustrated so that groups of three can study together. Give each group the task of comparing and contrasting the contributions of the illustrations in *The Water of Life* and the book each is sharing. Tell them to prepare a short presentation to the class in which they will point out the details in the illustrations that carry the story along. Remind them to study the borders carefully. Tell them to use the book as they share with the class and to show their examples. This may also be done as a written activity if desired. Keep the books together in one place in the room for further examination by interested students.

FOLLOW-UP ACTIVITIES FOR TEACHER AND STUDENTS TO SHARE:

1. Introduce *Anno's Aesop,* by Mitsumasa Anno, by sharing the information "About Aesop's Fables" that Anno has included at the close of the book. Then share the foreword, "Mr. Fox's Fables," below the table of contents. Read the first three fables, also reading Mr. Fox's version of each story found below the illustration.

   Now ask members of the class to pretend they can't read, to study one of Anno's pictures of a fable, and then to write a fable using the picture only. Be sure to use only a few characters, be brief, and give a moral. After writing the original fable, read Aesop's fable. Share both with the class as time allows.

2. Before reading Anno's *In Shadowland,* explain to the class that there are two related stories within the book, one illustrated in watercolor and the other in black using an Oriental papercut technique. Read the book in a normal way, thus alternating the stories. When the little match girl and the watchman run to Shadowland, ending the watercolor portion of the story, continue the shadow story to its conclusion. Examine the illustrations with the class. Do they seem appropriate for the content? Does anyone have an idea about the theme of the book?

   Now read aloud Hans Christian Andersen's *The Little Match Girl* illustrated by Rachel Isadora. Ask the class how the illustrations contribute to the mood of the story. Does the class prefer Andersen's story or Anno's interpretation?

   Would the class like to go to Shadowland and miss winter? Why or why not? Have everyone cut out a shadow picture of a favorite winter activity. Put them on an "In Shadowland" bulletin board.

3. Let students working in groups of two or three see if they can locate the pigs and letters on each page of Arthur Geisert's *Pigs from A to Z.* Which group can find the most?

   As a follow-up suggest that each group try to make a picture using letters of the alphabet. Post the pictures for other members of the class to examine.

4. Before reading Gerald McDermott's *Arrow to the Sun,* tell the class that McDermott received the Caldecott Medal in 1975 for the illustrations in this book, judged the most outstanding of any picture book published in the the United States in the previous year. Ask the class to examine the symbols as they hear the story. Let the class tell the part of the story in the textless pages that illustrate Boy's four trials.

   After reading the story, examine the illustrations again and let the class interpret the meaning of the symbols. Follow up by having the class paint or make a collage illustration of themselves as if they too were celebrating Boy's return by participating in the Dance of Life.

5. Before reading Gerald McDermott's *The Stonecutter,* explain to the students that the book is full of graphic symbols of the stages of transformation for the stonecutter. For example, the square within the circle symbolizes Tasaku's block of stone. They are to watch for others and try to interpret the meaning.

   After you have read the book to them, let the students discuss the symbols. Follow the discussion by showing the sound filmstrip *Evolution of a Graphic Concept: The Stonecutter* (Weston Woods, 1977). If it is not available in the school library, ask the librarian to obtain it on interlibrary loan. In the filmstrip McDermott explains the many symbols. After showing the filmstrip examine the illustrations in the book again. Talk about the symbols and the visual statements made by the illustrator. Why did he choose collage as the medium?

6. Before reading Harve Zemach's *Duffy and the Devil,* tell the class that it is a version of Rumpelstiltskin that was a popular play in Cornwall, England, in the nineteenth century. Margot Zemach received the Caldecott Medal for this book in 1974. Ask the class to look closely at the illustrations, as you read, to see if they provide clues to the country, the mood, and the characters in the story. After they have heard the story, ask them to examine the illustrations again and discuss life in Cornwall in the nineteenth century as presented by artist Margot Zemach.

   Ask a committee of students to go to the school library to find information about life today in Cornwall. Encyclopedias or travel books of England may be a good place to start. Have the students report to the class on how life in Cornwall has changed in the twentieth century.

FOLLOW-UP ACTIVITIES FOR INDIVIDUALS OR SMALL GROUPS:

1. Examine *Anno's Journey*. Locate the illustration of the Pied Piper of Hamelin, the Emperor from "The Emperor's New Clothes," Red Riding Hood, Pinocchio, and Don Quixote. Find a book about one of these characters in the school library. Read the book and share a favorite illustration with the class.
2. Study the illustrations in *Anno's Journey*. Make a list of illustrations that continue from page to page to complete a scene.
3. Examine *Anno's Italy* very carefully. Find Pinocchio, the Three Pigs, the Ugly Duckling, Ali Baba, Cinderella, and Strega Nona. Go to the school or public library and locate a story about Strega Nona. Share the story with the class.
4. Examine Tomie de Paola's illustrations in *The Hunter and the Animals*. What is the theme of the story? List the events in the plot that contributed to the development of the theme. Why do you think de Paola chose to present this theme in a textless picture book instead of in an essay?
5. Read Steven Kellogg's *Pecos Bill*. Now go back and examine the illustrations carefully. List five examples in the illustrations of the foreshadowing of coming events or of visual ideas that extend the humor of the story.
6. Read Marianna Mayer's version of *The Twelve Dancing Princesses*. Did the illustrations contribute to the understanding of character, plot, setting, and theme? If so, in what way? Did the borders add to the story? If so, in what way?
7. After a group of students have individually read the pictures in Lynd Ward's *The Silver Pony,* hold a book discussion with the teacher or librarian. Share your perception of the plot, characters, setting, and theme.
8. After hearing Harve Zemach's *Duffy and the Devil,* read Paul Zelinsky's *Rumpelstiltskin*. Then examine the illustrations in both books. Compare the two versions. Describe the different mood and characterization depicted in the two stories.

Exploring Poetry

STUDENT OBJECTIVES:

1. Notice rhythm, rhyme, sound, and imagery as elements of poetry.
2. Describe how the shape of concrete poetry strengthens the imagery.
3. Interpret poetry through choral reading.
4. Recognize narrative poems, limericks, free verse, and haiku as different forms of poetry.

RECOMMENDED READING:

Adoff, Arnold. *All the Colors of the Race.* Illustrated by John Steptoe. Lothrop, Lee & Shepard, 1982. (Objective 4)
Adoff's poems show the feelings of a child with a black mother and a white father.

Ciardi, John. *The Hopeful Trout and Other Limericks.* Illustrated by Susan Meddaugh. Houghton Mifflin, 1989. (Objective 4)
Forty humorous limericks will delight the reader.

Fleischman, Paul. *Joyful Noise.* Illustrated by Eric Beddows. Harper & Row, 1988. (Objective 3)
Two-part poems introduce the characteristics of many insects.

Fleischman, Paul. *I Am Phoenix.* Illustrated by Ken Nutt. Harper & Row, 1985. (Objective 3)
Bird poems to be read aloud by two people or groups.

Froman, Robert. *Seeing Things.* Thomas Y. Crowell, 1974, 1987. (Objective 2)
The fifty-one short poems are printed in shapes relevant to each poem's content.

Kuskin, Karla. *Dogs and Dragons, Trees and Dreams.* Harper & Row, 1980. (Objectives 1, 4)
The poet introduces many of her poems with notes which call attention to their rhythm, word sounds, and rhyme.

Livingston, Myra Cohn. *Celebrations.* Illustrated by Leonard Everett Fisher. Holiday House, 1985. (Objectives 1, 4)
Sixteen poems present the varying moods of the year's holidays.

Livingston, Myra Cohn. *A Circle of Seasons.* Illustrated by Leonard Everett Fisher. Holiday House, 1982. (Objective 1)
Imagery-filled poems celebrate the changing seasons.

Longfellow, Henry Wadsworth. *Paul Revere's Ride.* Illustrated by Nancy Winslow Parker. Greenwillow, 1985. (Objective 4)
A narrative poem recounts the famous ride to warn colonial American villagers and farmers that the British are coming.

Merriam, Eve. *A Sky Full of Poems.* Illustrated by Walter Gaffney-Kessell. Dell, 1986. paper. (Objectives 1, 3)
This collection of poems is filled with rhythm, rhyme, sound, and imagery.

Mizumura, Kazue. *Flower Moon Snow: A Book of Haiku.* Harper & Row, 1977. (Objective 4)
Simple woodcut illustrations enlarge the images in the thirty haiku poems of nature.

Prelutsky, Jack. *The Snopp on the Sidewalk and Other Poems.* Illustrated by Bryon Barton. Greenwillow, 1977. (Objectives 3, 4)
Twelve humorous poems depict imaginary creatures one might find around the neighborhood.

The Random House Book of Poetry for Children. Selected by Jack Prelutsky. Illustrated by Arnold Lobel. Random House, 1983. (Objectives 1, 4)
Prelutsky's anthology assembles 572 poems into fourteen sections, each introduced by a poem of his own.

Sandburg, Carl. *Rainbows Are Made.* Illustrated by Fritz Eichenberg. Harcourt Brace Jovanovich, 1982. (Objective 1)
Wood engravings enhance seventy poems on a variety of subjects.

GROUP INTRODUCTORY ACTIVITY:

Preparing for the Activity: Locate *The Random House Book of Poetry for Children,* selected by Jack Prelutsky. Read and familiarize yourself with the poems listed below. Have access to a chalkboard and overhead projector. Duplicate, as a transparency, Nikki Giovanni's poem (page 119 of the anthology).

Focus: Ask the students if they can tell you what a poem is. Most of the students will know that poems may rhyme—some will think poems *must rhyme.* During the discussion, mention the rhythm and imagery in poetry if the students do not. Explain that poems may take different forms such as narrative poetry, limericks, free verse, and haiku.

Objective: To satisfy the objective of noticing rhythm, rhyme, sound, and imagery, and to recognize forms of poetry: narratives, limericks, and free verse, introduce *The Random House Book of Poetry for Children.* Tell the students that you will read poems that have the elements of rhythm, rhyme, sound, and imagery. Write those words on the board or an overhead transparency, leaving space for titles of poems underneath. Explain that as you read, the students' task is to find those elements and be ready to discuss them. Write *Limerick, Narrative,* and *Free verse,* and explain that you will teach these terms as well.

Guided Activity: Read "Lone Dog," by Irene McLeod, page 65 of the anthology. Lead the students to the elements of sound, rhythm, and rhyme. Ask how the internal rhyme—rhyming words in the same line—adds to the sound enjoyment. Discuss the rhythm of the short, explosive words. Talk about consonant sounds and vowel sounds. Do the students think that the poet chose her sounds for any reason? What reason? Write this title under *Sound, Rhythm,* and *Rhyme* on the chalkboard or overhead transparency.

Read the limericks, "Hog-Calling Competition" by Morris Bishop and "There Was an Old Man with a Beard" by Edward Lear, on page 163 of the anthology. Explain that the Lear limerick follows the tradition of beginning with the phrase, "There was a . . ." Ask the students to note how many lines are in the limerick, how many rhymes, and how the rhymes are arranged. Have them clap the rhythm, and call their attention to the difference between the five lines. Note that the Lear poem has been printed as four lines, but should be divided between "hen" and "four." Write the titles under *Limerick.*

Read "The Reason I Like Chocolate" by Nikki Giovanni, page 119. Ask what the students heard that was different about this poem. Lead them to the fact that the poem has no rhyme and no strongly identifiable rhythm. Ask the students which poetry form they would expect this to be—narrative, limerick, or free verse—and why. Show them the poem on the overhead, and ask how it resembles other poems. Write this title under *Free verse* on the board.

Read "Buffalo Dusk" by Carl Sandburg, page 58. Ask the students to identify the sight imagery in the short poem. How does the repeating of the word "great" add to the imagery? Why did Sandburg repeat it? Why does he repeat the word "gone"? Ask the students to identify the form of the poem. They should recognize it as a free verse, with the word "gone" repeated at the ends of the lines. Write this title under *Free Verse* and *Imagery.*

Read "The Four Seasons" by Jack Prelutsky, anthology page 35. Ask the students to identify the sight imagery in this poem, which is designed to introduce the next poems. How does the poet describe each season with sight imagery? Have the students search for color words. Identify imagery that identifies each season. Ask the students to decide why the seasons are a suitable topic to describe using imagery. Write this title under *Imagery.*

Before reading "Jabberwocky" by Lewis Carroll, page 178, explain that many of the words are nonsense words that Carroll invented for this poem, but that the students should be able to create a story they feel is told in the poem. Introduce the poem by telling the students that this poem is included in the book *Through the Looking Glass* by Lewis Carroll. When finished, ask if anyone can relate the details of the story of the Jabberwock. They may say that a young boy is warned that the Jabberwock is dangerous, but he searches with his sword anyway. As he is resting against a tree, the Jabberwock suddenly appears. With two swipes, the boy kills the beast and returns home with its head. At home he is greeted with great joy, and the world seems to return to the serenity of pre-Jabberwock days. To make the students feel more secure, tell them that in the book, Alice is unsure of the meaning of the poem. Tell them that she says that "somehow, it seems to fill her head with ideas—only she doesn't exactly know what they are! However, *somebody* killed *something*."

Ask the students if they can explain why this is a narrative poem. Lead them to the understanding of narrative as telling a story. Discuss the sounds of the words, and the rhyming pattern. Repeat some of the stanzas, this time concentrating on the sounds of the nonsense words. If there is time, let the students guess at the meanings of some of the words. Point out that "chortle" is now a word in the dictionary, even though Carroll invented it for this poem. Write this title under *Narrative, Rhyme,* and *Sound.*

Extending Activity: Make the book and other poetry collections available for reading during class silent reading times. Have students find other examples of narrative, free verse, and limerick forms. Begin a class list of poetry forms, and ask students to contribute titles when they find poems that demonstrate the forms. Ask them to become aware of sounds, imagery, rhyme, and rhythm in poetry. Let all the students find and read favorite examples to one another, to you, and to the principal. Have them explain which elements they enjoy. Use snatches of time during the day to read and recite favorite poems. Keep poetry in front of the students every day.

FOLLOW-UP ACTIVITIES FOR TEACHER AND STUDENTS TO SHARE:

1. Introduce Arnold Adoff's *All the Colors of the Race* by saying this poetry is free verse with no rhyme. The importance of each poem is the emotion and message presented. Read "If they hate me" and "For everyone." Let students talk about the meaning of each of those two poems.

   Read "Stop looking." Urge the class to make other couplet verses with the same message. Read "Remember" and "I was Harriet." Who was the poem about? Suggest that someone find out more in the library about Harriet Tubman and share the information with the class.

2. Introduce John Ciardi's *The Hopeful Trout and Other Limericks* by reviewing with the class the limerick form—a five-line verse

with an *aabba* rhyme scheme. Suggest to the class that they listen to the rhythm as you read several poems.

Look at the title. As a class, make a limerick about a hopeful trout. Now read Ciardi's trout limerick, on page 13 of his book. Read a few more of Ciardi's poems so students sense that the last line usually gives some humorous twist to the poem.

As a follow-up ask each child to write a limerick, illustrate it, and share it with the class. If possible, duplicate the page each child prepares and make a book of limericks for each member of the class.

3. To introduce Paul Fleischman's *Joyful Noise,* tell the class that the book won Fleischman the Newbery Medal in 1989 as the most distinguished book for children published in the United States during the previous year. Explain that these are two-part poems. One person reads the left-hand part and the other reads the right-hand part. At times they read separately but if both parts are printed in the same line across, they are spoken in unison.

Ahead of time have one of the students practice "Grasshoppers" with you. Read it aloud to the class. Also ahead of time prepare "Water Striders" on a transparency. Divide the class in half and read it as a choral. Read it twice so everyone in the class gets the idea of how the poems are read.

Introduce Paul Fleischman's *I Am Phoenix,* also composed of poems for two voices. Suggest that those who wish may choose a partner, practice a poem from one of the two books, and read it to the class.

4. Introduce Robert Froman's *Seeing Things* by asking the class if they know what concrete poetry is. If no one has an accurate definition, explain that it is poetry that is arranged on the page in a shape that depicts the subject, or topic, of the poem.

Read "Box of Words" without giving the title or showing the shape. Ask the class if they can suggest a title or the shape. Now reveal Froman's title and shape for the poem. Read "Dead Tree." As before, do not give the title or show the shape. After reading the poem let the class suggest appropriate titles and shapes. Compare the type used for "Box of Words" with the letters used in "Dead Tree." Why was there a difference?

Read "Wall Walk." Then let the class suggest the shape. Show them "Graveyard" and "Cumulus." Ask each member of the class to read other poems from Froman's book as they wish and write a concrete poem to share with the class. Compile their poems into a book for the classroom reading table.

5. Read the class Karla Kuskin's introductory notes in *Dogs and Dragons, Trees and Dreams* before reading aloud the poems they preface. Read "Thistles." Read it again, asking the class to listen for favorite sounds. Let them share the words they heard. After

reading the introduction to the poem, ask the class to close their eyes as you read "Full of the Moon." Read "A Dance," asking the class to notice the varied rhythm in the verses.

Tell the class that "A Bug Sat in a Silver Flower" is a narrative poem that tells a story. Read the short poem and let the class recall the story.

Suggest that members of the class may want to find a favorite poem in this book, practice reading it, and read it to the teacher to get suggestions before sharing it with the class.

6. Introduce Myra Livingston's *A Circle of Seasons* by telling the class that Livingston often uses action words to present the imagery. Read "Spring brings out her baseball bat." See if anyone remembers the imagery introduced by baseball terms. If needed, read the poem again before discussing the imagery.

Read "Summer blasts off fireworks." Notice Leonard Fisher's illustration. How does it add to the mood of the poem? Before reading "Autumn calls the winning toss," let the class suggest what sport will provide the action words for the imagery. Ask the class to listen for the word pictures so they can talk about them after hearing the poem.

Complete the seasons with "Winter etches windowpanes." Again, discuss the imagery after the poem is read.

7. Introduce Eve Merriam's *A Sky Full of Poems* by reading "Double Trouble." Before reading the poem, ask the class to notice the rhyme, sounds, and imagery it contains. After reading the poem, talk about its rhyme. How does the class usually think of poems rhyming? What is different about this poem's rhyme? Reread the poem. Talk about the humor in the lines.

To read "A Round" divide the class in half. One group will say "spaghetti," the other group will say "spaghetti," then the teacher will read line 3. Point to each group so they need not practice. Before reading "Winter Alphabet," ask the class to listen for words that make pictures in their minds. Read the short poem twice. Then let the class talk about the imagery.

Ahead of time read Merriam's thoughts on "Writing a Poem." Share with the class the process by which her poem evolved. Suggest that members of the class read other poems in the book as they find time. If they find one they particularly like, they may want to copy it and illustrate it for a bulletin board. Be sure that any copied poems give credit to the poet and the title of the book from which it came.

8. Before reading Kazue Mizumura's *Flower Moon Snow,* share the ideas in the introduction in which she explains the technique of writing haiku. Read a number of the poems, giving the class time to examine the woodcut illustrations.

As a follow-up take the class on a walk. Let the students each use a 35 mm camera to take a picture of something in nature that intrigues them about which they can write a haiku.

After the film is developed, let each class member attach his or her photograph to a sheet of white paper and copy the haiku he or she has written beneath the picture.

9. Introduce Jack Prelutsky's *The Snopp on the Sidewalk* by telling the class that the title poem is a narrative poem that tells a story. Read the poem. Let the class recount the story told in the poem. How did the poem make them feel? Was it funny or sad?

   Read "Wrimples." Let the class think of other things a wrimple might do. As a group create new verses for the poem. Call the children's attention to the *abab* rhyme scheme.

   Read "The Groobles." What was the climax of the poem? Ahead of time prepare "Splatt" on a transparency. Tell the class that this is a tongue twister. Read it together. Then read it three times, each time a little faster than the last.

10. Introduce the rhythm in Carl Sandburg's poetry by reading "Was Ever a Dream a Drum" and "Paper I" from *Rainbows Are Made*. Tell the class that many of Sandburg's poems are full of imagery. Suggest that "Fog" is a poem very familiar to many. Tell them to listen to the word pictures very carefully. You will read it twice, then see if the class can recall it enough to join in on the third reading. Now see if anyone can say it alone. After a few have tried, say it again as a group.

   Tell the class that Gene Kelly was a popular movie star of the past who was a dancer. Suggest you will read the poem "Lines Written for Gene Kelly To Dance To" so they get the idea. Then you will ask for volunteers to dance or pantomime the poem as you read it again.

   Suggest that as the students hear the poems during the unit, class members should keep in mind and make note of their favorites. They may want to plan a poetry program to share with parents or another class.

FOLLOW-UP ACTIVITIES FOR INDIVIDUALS OR SMALL GROUPS:

1. Read the five untitled poems on pages 64–69 of Karla Kuskin's *Dogs and Dragons, Trees and Dreams*. Write a title for each poem.
2. Read "Memorial Day" and "Fourth of July" from Myra Livingston's *Celebrations*. Why is there a difference in the mood of the two poems? Write a limerick recalling a Fourth of July celebration.
3. Read Henry Wadsworth Longfellow's *Paul Revere's Ride* illustrated by Nancy Parker. In a paragraph tell the story presented in the poem.
4. Read Jack Prelutsky's *The Snopp on the Sidewalk* again after hearing it in class. Cut gray yarn into 6-inch pieces and tie in

the middle with thread. Make a little snopp, creating eyes and mouth from cloth or paper.
5. Read "Arithmetic" from Carl Sandburg's *Rainbows Are Made.* Write a parody of this poem named "Geography."

Analyzing Contemporary Realistic Fiction

STUDENT OBJECTIVES:

1. Decide whether the story has an interesting, believable plot that centers around a problem young people could really have.
2. Identify round characters with positive and negative qualities that help the reader understand why they act as they do.
3. Determine the theme that gives the reader something to think about after the story is read.
4. Assess whether the story has a readable style that makes the reader want to complete the book.
5. Share a scene or character with the class to make them want to read the book.
6. Analyze the literary qualities of a book that won the Newbery Medal for the author.
7. Decide whether the point of view was appropriate and how the book would have been changed with a different point of view.

RECOMMENDED READING:

Bunting, Eve. *Is Anybody There?* J.B. Lippincott, 1988. (Objectives 1, 2, 4)
A latchkey child solves the mystery of the disappearance of items from the house.

Byars, Betsy. *Cracker Jackson.* Viking, 1985. (Objectives 1, 5)
Jackson tries to save his ex-babysitter from physical abuse by her husband.

Byars, Betsy. *The Summer of the Swans.* Illustrated by Ted CoConis. Viking, 1970. (Objectives 2, 3, 4, 6)
Sara is filled with self-pity until her ten-year-old retarded brother disappears and the search brings everything back into perspective.

Calhoun, Mary. *Julie's Tree.* Harper & Row, 1988. (Objectives 1, 4, 5)
Julie goes to live with her father, and through trying to save a tree, she makes new friends.

Cleary, Beverly. *Dear Mr. Henshaw.* Illustrated by Paul Zelinsky. William Morrow, 1983. (Objectives 1, 5, 6)
Leigh is helped in coping with his parents' divorce by writing to his favorite author.

Garrigue, Sheila. *Between Friends.* Bradbury, 1978. (Objectives 1, 2)
Jill makes friends with a girl with Down's syndrome, and that causes her problems with other supposed friends.

Konigsburg, E. L. *Throwing Shadows.* Atheneum, 1979. (Objectives 1, 2, 3, 7)
Five first-person short stories in which boys learn more about their own personalities.

McDonald, Joyce. *Mail-Order Kid.* G. P. Putnam's Sons, 1988. (Objectives 1, 2, 4, 5)
Ten-year-old Flip's problems with his mail-order fox help him to understand his adopted Korean brother.

McKenna, Colleen O'Shaughnessy. *Fourth Grade Is a Jinx.* Scholastic, 1988. (Objectives 1, 5)
Collette is embarrassed when her mother becomes the substitute teacher for her class.

Paterson, Katherine. *Bridge to Terabithia.* Illustrated by Donna Diamond. Thomas Y. Crowell, 1977. (Objectives 2, 3, 6)
Jess, a ten-year-old boy, profits from his friendship with Leslie and their creation of an imaginary land.

Paterson, Katherine. *The Great Gilly Hopkins.* Thomas Y. Crowell, 1978. (Objectives 1, 2, 5, 7)
An eleven-year-old foster child copes with her feelings of desperation by scheming against those who want to help her.

Slote, Alfred. *Moving In.* J. B. Lippincott, 1988. (Objectives 1, 2, 4)
Eleven-year-old Robbie and his older sister Peggy scheme to deter their widowed father from marrying his new business partner, Ruth.

Smith, Doris Buchanan. *A Taste of Blackberries.* Thomas Y. Crowell, 1973. (Objectives 1, 2, 3, 4, 5, 7)
A boy learns to cope with death when a close friend dies.

Stolz, M. S. *A Dog on Barkham Street.* Illustrated by Leonard Shortall. Harper & Row, 1960. (Objectives 1, 2, 3, 4, 7)
Edward wants two things: to be rid of the bully next door and to have a dog.

Stolz, Mary. *The Bully of Barkham Street.* Illustrated by Leonard Shortall. Harper & Row, 1963. (Objectives 1, 2, 3, 4, 7)
Describes the conflict in *A Dog on Barkham Street* from Martin's rather than Edward's viewpoint.

GROUP INTRODUCTORY ACTIVITY:

Preparing for the Activity: Locate E. L. Konigsburg's short story collection, *Throwing Shadows.* Read the first story, "On Shark's Tooth Beach."

Focus: Ask the students if they can do something that makes them feel proud. Let them explore these skills with questions like: "Where did you learn that? How did you improve? Did someone teach you? Could you teach it to someone else? Would you want to teach it to someone else? How does it make you special? How do you feel if you find somebody who has the same skills you do? Do you want to be the best, or do you feel glad that they are good, too?"

Objective: This activity is designed to satisfy the objectives of deciding whether the story has a believable plot, identifying round characters, determining if the theme gives readers something to think about, and deciding whether the point of view is appropriate. Tell the students that you will read a short story about a young boy who has a special talent for finding fossilized sharks' teeth. Make sure that the students understand what "fossilized" means. Explain that Ned will encounter a person who makes him think about his skill in a new way. Tell them that you want them to listen for the relationship between Ned and President Bob. How do they really feel about each other? Say that you will ask for their idea of the theme—what Ned learns in the story.

Guided Activity: Read the first page of "On Shark's Tooth Beach," by Konigsburg. Stop and ask if the students can tell you who is telling the story and how they know. Describe this as first person point of view—a character *in* the story is telling the story as he or she sees it or recalls it. Explore some of the problems this point of view would give an author (one person's ideas only for what's happening, only one person's thoughts). Help the students to realize that the reader of a first person point of view must be careful in accepting the ideas of the narrator—or person telling the story. The reader must be wary because there may be times when the narrator doesn't see or know everything he or she might need to in order to understand fully what is happening and what that might mean. Tell them to listen very carefully as Ned tells his side of the story.

Continue reading and finish the story. You may need to explain the allusion to Sampson and the jawbone. Tell the students that Sampson, a character in the Bible, fought an entire army of well-armed men with just the bone from the jaw of a donkey. Ask how, if "smite" means "to hit," does Ned want to "smite" President Bob? How could he smite President Bob? Why?

Explore the characters of Ned and President Bob. What details show them both as round, well-developed characters? What are some of the positive and the negative traits of each? How do the students know about Ned's negative traits if he doesn't tell them to the reader? What is Ned's problem in this story? How does he make it better or worse? Why is President Bob such a problem? What does he do to make the problem worse? Why does he act the way he does? Does he seem to have anyone else to talk to? Could there be a reason for this? Why do the two characters seem to compete over finding the teeth? Why is it important to Ned that he always have the best or the most or the biggest?

Ask the students to share their ideas about the theme of the story. What does Ned learn about people and himself in this experience? Will he act differently in the future?

At the end Ned says that he doesn't want to put words to the picture of his face. What does he mean? Have the students think of a movie title that would describe Ned's face before and after he gave the trophy. Why did Ned give the jawbone to President Bob? Ask if the students were surprised when Ned did that.

Extending Activity: Review the final scene in the story. Let each of the students choose one of the other characters who was present at this scene—Ned's mother or President Bob. Ask the students to rewrite this scene from the first-person point of view of the mother or the old man. Remind them that they must pretend to be that character, and they will only know what that character can see or hear or feel. Remind them to use first-person pronouns like "I, me, my" when they are referring to their character. When the class is finished writing, have them share their retellings in small groups. Have the groups discuss the difficulties of writing in the first person.

Individual Activity: Suggest that students read others of the stories in this collection. Tell them that all the stories are written in first person point of view, and that the characters each learn something important about themselves in the stories. Have the students share with the class the stories that they read, discussing character, theme, and point of view.

FOLLOW-UP ACTIVITIES FOR TEACHER AND STUDENTS TO SHARE:

1. Introduce Eve Bunting's *Is Anybody There?* by asking the class if they know what the term "latchkey kid" means. Ask them what problems a child on his or her own at home might face. Tell them this is a mystery story of a boy who tries to solve the problem of why items are disappearing from the house. Suggest that those in the class who like mysteries read the story. Ask each to write a paragraph telling whether the situation was realistic. Why or why not? If several in the class read the book,

have a small group discussion of the realism of the plot, the characterization, and the style. Did the book keep them wanting to continue until the end?

2. Introduce Betsy Byars' *Cracker Jackson* by telling the class that a boy knows that his ex-babysitter is being abused by her husband. He takes it upon himself to do something about it.

   Ask two boys in the class to read the book and introduce it to the class with the telephone call between Goat and Jackson, from page 11 to the top of page 14 when the conversation is cut off. Have the two class members make a script of the phone conversation and read it to the class, pretending to be talking on the telephone. After their introduction let the class suggest possible ways Jackson can help Alma.

3. Before reading Betsy Byars' *The Summer of the Swans,* show the class the sound filmstrip *Meet the Newbery Author: Betsy Byars* (Random House, 1978). If it is not available in the school or public library, ask the librarian to borrow it on interlibrary loan. After they have watched the filmstrip, ask the class if Byars is an author they would like to meet. What would they ask her?

   Before reading Byars' *The Summer of the Swans,* tell the class that she won the Newbery Medal in 1971 for this book. Explain that you are going to read the book aloud without discussion. Then as a class they will discuss Sara's problem, Sara's character traits, the theme of the book, elements of style, and whether they feel the author deserved the Newbery Medal for this book. After the book is completed, hold such a discussion with the class.

4. Introduce Mary Calhoun's *Julie's Tree* by reading Chapter 1. Does the class feel it has a realistic style that makes one want to continue? Is Julie's problem believable?

   Ask three members of the class to read the book and then make a script from the scene, pages 38–40, when Julie and Ned are ordered out of the tree. Have them read their script to the class. Does the class have any ideas about what will happen?

5. Introduce Joyce McDonald's *Mail-Order Kid* by reading Chapter 1. Let the class discuss Flip's problem with his mail-order fox. Does the mother's action seem realistic? What clues are there to Flip's attitude toward his younger brother? Does that seem realistic? Does the style of writing make one want to continue reading? What does the class think will happen in Chapter 2? Let the class characterize Flip as they know him thus far.

   Ask for two volunteers to read the book. In their report to the class, ask them to be Flip and Todd telling the class about their problems.

6. Introduce Colleen McKenna's *Fourth Grade Is a Jinx* by telling the class that Collette thinks she has a problem when her mother becomes the substitute teacher for Collette's class. Ask two members of the class to read the book and share the scene on

pages 52 and 53 when Collette's mother tells her about the substitute job. They can either make it into a script and read the scene or become familiar enough with it to play it out without a script.

After hearing the scene, have the class discuss whether Collette's reaction was realistic. Would they have reacted in the same or a different way? Encourage others to read the book to find out how Collette and her mother solved their problem.

7. Introduce Katherine Paterson's *Bridge to Terabithia* by telling the class that this book won Paterson the Newbery Medal in 1978. Read Chapters 1 and 2 to the class. Then have the class characterize Jess and Leslie. Are they round characters? Have the class document the reasons for decisions they make about character traits.

   Read Chapters 3 and 4. Can the class add character traits now? What has the class learned about life in rural Virginia? Is the setting integral and important to the story? After reading Chapter 6 discuss the conflict. Is it self against self, self against another, self against nature, or self against society? Document the decision. After Chapter 8 see if the class can sense any foreshadowing.

   After the book is completed, the class may want to add to their discussion of conflict. Ask them to document whether Jess was a dynamic character—one who changed. What was the theme? Was the book realistic? In what ways? Did Paterson deserve the Newbery medal for this book? Why or why not?

8. Introduce Katherine Paterson's *The Great Gilly Hopkins* to the class after having read *Bridge to Terabithia*. Tell the class that Paterson wrote both books and that *The Great Gilly Hopkins* was a Newbery Honor book. Even though Paterson did not win the Newbery Medal for this book, it was recognized as a distinguished book. After reading Chapter 1, let the class talk about the problems a foster child faces. Is Gilly's reaction realistic?

   Show the class the sound filmstrip *Meet the Newbery Author: Katherine Paterson* (Random House, 1982), if you can borrow it from the school library or obtain it through interlibrary loan. Does knowing about the author help interest the class in reading her books? Urge members of the class who are interested to read *The Great Gilly Hopkins* and do one of the individual activities.

9. Introduce Alfred Slote's *Moving In* by reading the first four pages. Let the students guess what the conflict will be. After they predict, tell them that the father is a widower and the children try to keep him from a romance with his business partner Ruth. Let them predict what schemes the kids might use to discourage their father. Does the story seem realistic? Is the style thus far one that will keep you reading?

Ask two students to read the book, then share the schemes with the class. After sharing the schemes see if the class can characterize Robby and Peggy. Do they understand why the two acted as they did?

10. Introduce Doris Smith's *A Taste of Blackberries* to a small reading group by reading Chapter 1. Call attention to the figurative language. Ask that each member of the group complete the book in preparation for a small group discussion of conflict, style, characterization, and theme. Ask that they each look for an example of figurative language that they liked.

    After each member of the group has finished the book, have a small group discussion. Use terms shared in the group introductory activity and ask the class to document their responses with examples from the book. Did the class like the book being written in first person? Why or why not? How would the book have been different with a third-person point of view?

11. Introduce Mary S. Stolz's *A Dog on Barkham Street* by reading Chapter 1. Ask the class to identify Edward's problems and determine whether the book is realistic. Have them characterize Edward and defend their decisions. Does the story have a style that will make the reader want to continue? How would the class characterize Martin?

    On the following day read Chapter 2 of Stolz's *The Bully of Barkham Street.* Let the class recall their characterizations of Martin and Edward. Do they want to change any of their views now? How does the class think Edward and Martin will resolve their problem?

    Select a small reading group and ask half of them to read *A Dog on Barkham Street* and the other half to read *The Bully of Barkham Street.* Since these two stories recount the same incidents from opposing points of view, the joint group discussion after the two groups have read their respective books should be dynamic. Have them characterize Edward and Martin, decide on a theme, and talk about whether Martin's and Edward's problems were resolved. Will they ever become friends? Why or why not?

FOLLOW-UP ACTIVITIES FOR INDIVIDUALS OR SMALL GROUPS:

1. Read Betsy Byars' *Cracker Jackson.* Write a paragraph telling whether you think Jackson's attempt to drive the car to take Alma out of town was realistic. Why or why not?

2. Read Beverly Cleary's *Dear Mr. Henshaw.* Write a paragraph telling whether the ending seemed true to life. Would you have preferred a different ending? If so, what would it be? If not, why not?

3. Read Beverly Cleary's *Dear Mr. Henshaw*. Think about how the book would be different if it had been written from an *omniscient* point of view—the view as if the author knew what everyone was thinking and reported it. Do you prefer first person, the point of view Cleary *did* use, or would an omniscient point of view have been a better choice? Defend your answer.

4. Read Beverly Cleary's *Dear Mr. Henshaw*. The author won the Newbery Medal for this book in 1984. Do you feel the book deserved to win the author the medal? Justify your answer.

5. Read Beverly Cleary's *Dear Mr. Henshaw* and ask a friend to read it also. Make a script from the telephone call on pages 68–72. Read it to the class to introduce the book. Have the class discuss what the scene tells them about the characters.

6. Read Beverly Cleary's *Dear Mr. Henshaw*. Write a paragraph telling why the plot does or does not seem believable. Was Mr. Henshaw justified in answering Leigh's first letter the way he did? Make three rules about writing letters to authors.

7. Read Sheila Garrigue's *Between Friends*. Write a paragraph identifying the problems Jill's friendship with Dede caused? Would you characterize Jill as brave? Justify (give your reasons for) your answer.

8. Read Sheila Garrigue's *Between Friends*. Write a paragraph saying why you think the book is or is not realistic.

9. After hearing Katherine Paterson's *Bridge to Terabithia,* draw a picture of Terabithia.

10. Read Katherine Paterson's *The Great Gilly Hopkins*. Write a paragraph indicating whether the Courtney you met in the last chapter looked and acted in the way you expected her to look and act. Justify your answer. Did Paterson foreshadow the real character of Courtney? If so, in what way? Did you feel the ending was realistic? Justify your answer.

11. Read Katherine Paterson's *The Great Gilly Hopkins*. Write a paragraph on how the book would have been different if it were written from a different point of view.

12. Read Katherine Paterson's *The Great Gilly Hopkins*. Ask a friend to read the book. Together prepare a script of Gilly's meeting Agnes Stokes, pages 26–28. Read the scene to the class.

13. After reading Doris Smith's *A Taste of Blackberries* and hearing Katherine Paterson's *Bridge to Terabithia,* write a paragraph comparing and contrasting the two boys' reactions to the death of a close friend.

14. After reading Doris Smith's *A Taste of Blackberries,* work with three others who have read the book and make a play out of the hitchhiking scene. Share with the class.

Learning from Biographies and Autobiographies

STUDENT OBJECTIVES:

1. Determine whether the character is developed enough to allow the reader to understand the reasons for the subject's actions.
2. Determine whether any events in the subject's life caused him or her to write specific books.
3. Identify elements of style that make the biography or autobiography appealing.
4. Know the difference between a biography and an autobiography.

RECOMMENDED READING:

Bulla, Clyde Robert. *A Grain of Wheat: A Writer Begins.* David R. Godine, 1985. (Objectives 1, 3, 4)
   The author describes his boyhood on a Missouri farm and shows what influenced his early decision to be a writer.

Cleary, Beverly. *A Girl from Yamhill.* William Morrow, 1988. (Objectives 1, 2, 4)
   The author shares with readers her childhood life in Yamhill, Oregon, her high school days, and events that heightened her interest in writing.

Collins, David R. *The Country Artist: A Story about Beatrix Potter.* Illustrated by Karen Ritz. Carolrhoda, 1989. (Objectives 1, 2, 3, 4)
   Describes the life of the author/artist and why her books came to be.

Collins, David R. *To the Point: A Story about E. B. White.* Illustrated by Amy Johnson. Carolrhoda, 1989. (Objectives 1, 2, 3, 4)
   Presents E. B. White's childhood in New York, his decisions about a writing career, and the reasons his books for children were created.

Fritz, Jean. *Homesick: My Own Story.* Illustrated by Margaret Tomes. G. P. Putnam's Sons, 1982. (Objective 1)
   In this work of autobiographical fiction, the author depicts her childhood in China.

Hyman, Trina Schart. *Self-Portrait: Trina Schart Hyman.* Harper & Row, 1981. (Objectives 1, 2, 3, 4)
   The artist discusses her early life, her love of fairy tales, and her experiences in art.

Kamen, Gloria. *Kipling, Storyteller of East and West.* Atheneum, 1985. (Objectives 1, 2)
Describes Kipling's early life in India, his education in England, and jobs influencing his writing career.

Little, Jean. *Little by Little: A Writer's Childhood.* Viking, 1988. (Objectives 1, 2, 3, 4)
The author tells of the rejection and ridicule she suffered as a nearly blind child and how her love of books helped her overcome difficulties and become a writer.

Peet, Bill. *Bill Peet: An Autobiography.* Houghton Mifflin, 1989. (Objectives 2, 3, 4)
The author/illustrator explains the influences that caused him to begin his children's book career in 1959.

Quackenbush, Robert. *Mark Twain? What Kind of Name Is That?* Prentice-Hall, 1984. (Objectives 1, 2, 3, 4)
Cartoon illustrations add to the description of many jobs that helped shape Twain's writing career.

Stevenson, James. *Higher on the Door.* Greenwillow, 1987. (Objectives 3, 4)
As a grandfather the author recalls village life in the 1930s.

Stevenson, James. *When I Was Nine.* Greenwillow, 1986. (Objectives 3, 4)
The author recalls school, friends, publishing a weekly neighborhood paper, and childhood vacation fun.

Zemach, Margot. *Self-Portrait: Margot Zemach.* Harper & Row, 1978. (Objectives 1, 2, 3, 4)
Illustrations from Zemach's books enhance her story of her life and the events that influenced her to choose illustrating children's books as a career.

GROUP INTRODUCTORY ACTIVITY:

Preparing for the Activity: Locate David Collins' *The Country Artist: A Story about Beatrix Potter.* Have several of Potter's books on hand to show the students. If possible, also locate the filmstrip *Meet the Author: Beatrix Potter Had a Pet Named Peter* (Random House, 1984) for the extending activity.

Focus: Ask the students if they have ever felt that they do not have enough freedom, if they feel like lots of decisions are made at home without their being able to share their feelings. Let the students discuss areas of their lives where they seem to have little control. Ask them to talk about how it feels to be "put down" and not listened to. Ask how they would feel if they could not play with their friends.

Now tell the students that one of the most famous artists and authors of children's books led a life much like the one you have been discussing—that she never had friends, that she was alone in her room for most of the time, that her parents told her what to do when they were not too busy with their own lives to ignore her. Tell the students that this describes the life of Beatrix Potter. Pause to see if the students recognize her name. Show several of her books, and share the titles of others. Ask what kind of childhood they would have expected the author and illustrator of *The Tale of Peter Rabbit* to have had. Why is it a surprise that she was treated poorly by her parents?

Objective: This activity is designed to satisfy the objectives of knowing the difference between a biography and an autobiography, understanding a subject's actions, determining whether events in the author's life caused her to write specific books, and determining elements of style that make a book readable. Tell the students that you will read portions of a biography about Beatrix Potter. It is a biography rather than an autobiography because it was written about Beatrix Potter, not *by* Beatrix Potter. If she had written about her own life it would have been an autobiography.

As you read, you are asking the students to listen to events in her life that brought her pleasure, and how she entertained herself. Compare and contrast her childhood with that of children today. Tell them that you will not read the entire book, but that they may wish to complete it on their own.

Guided Activity: Read the first chapter of Collins' *The Country Artist* to the class. Remind them that they are to be listening for some of her early interests and enjoyments. When you have completed this chapter, ask the students to list the pleasures in young Beatrix's life. How did those pleasures affect her later work as an author and illustrator? What traits of Beatrix's do they admire? Why? How did members of Beatrix's family and the servants act toward her? Ask the students to consider the style of the book. What makes the biography appeal to the reader? Return to page 13 and reread the second paragraph. Have the students find imagery. Does it help them picture the setting?

Ask if they think Collins was reporting all the words of the characters exactly, or if he was imagining what could have been said? Why would a biographer make up conversations between the subjects in a book? How does conversation add to the work?

Extending Activity: Return to the first paragraph of the book and reread it to the students. Ask them to explain how the author got their attention right away. Tell them to think of how they could write about their own life in such an interesting way, particularly in the first sentence. Have the students write an introductory paragraph of an autobiography. The paragraph should attract the reader's interest and make the reader want to know more. Let the students read their paragraphs to the class or to partners. Collect and display the work.

If possible, show the sound filmstrip *Meet the Author: Beatrix Potter Had a Pet Named Peter* (Random House, 1984). Ask the students to compare information in the filmstrip and the chapter read.

Ask volunteers to finish this book and to read at least one of Potter's books. Tell the students that anyone who does complete the book can participate in a book discussion about Potter's life and her work. After the book discussion ask someone to report to the class about Potter's later life, and her efforts to preserve the countryside.

Let a group of students prepare a timeline of the important events and works in Potter's life. Display the timeline.

FOLLOW-UP ACTIVITIES FOR TEACHER AND STUDENTS TO SHARE:

1. Introduce Clyde Robert Bulla's autobiography *A Grain of Wheat* by reading pages 1 and 2. Talk about the meaning of biography and autobiography. Tell students that the book is a partial autobiography because it covers only Bulla's childhood.

   Suggest that someone read the book and one of the books from the school or public library that Bulla has written. Ask them to share with the class Bulla's character traits seen from events in his boyhood and how he became a writer at age ten. Ask them to talk about Bulla's writing style in his autobiography and the story they read by him.

2. Introduce Beverly Cleary's autobiography *A Girl from Yamhill* by asking if anyone has read *Henry Huggins* or any of the *Ramona* books. Ask someone to read Part I of the autobiography and describe Cleary's early life in Yamhill to the class. Was there anything in her early life that influenced her career as an author? Characterize the child Beverly Cleary.

3. Introduce the biography by David Collins *To the Point: A Story about E. B. White* by asking how many students have read or heard the book *Charlotte's Web*. Explain that *To the Point* is about that book's author, E. B. White. Read the paragraph on page 17 beginning with "Yes, words strung together are like a necklace." Let the class discuss the meaning. Suggest that someone read the biography and White's *Charlotte's Web* (Harper & Row, 1952). If that person has read *Charlotte's Web,* he or she may want to read White's *Stuart Little* (Harper & Row, 1945). Ask the student to tell the class about White's character traits, about the steps in his becoming a writer of children's books, and about his reasons for writing *Charlotte's Web* or *Stuart Little.* Was the style of the biography appealing to the reader? Why or why not?

4. Introduce Jean Fritz's *Homesick: My Own Story* by reading the foreword, which tells why the book is classified as fiction. Ask the class if anyone has read one of Fritz's biographies of American heroes that has a "question" title, such as *Where Do You Think You're Going, Christopher Columbus?* Read Chapter 1 of *Homesick*. Have the class characterize Jean.

   Ask class members to read *Homesick* and one of the biographies Jean Fritz has written. Tell them that when they report to the class they should be sure to describe her feelings about returning to the United States and the way she was treated in school. Also, they should discuss her style of writing in her biographies. Was it different from *Homesick?*

5. Introduce Trina Schart Hyman by telling the class that Trina has won the Caldecott Medal for her illustrations in *Saint George and the Dragon*. Share with the class the first four pages, "The Farm," from her autobiography *Self-Portrait*. Ask them to listen for figurative language such as "old fierce boxwood trees." After reading the short section, talk about the figurative language. What can the class tell you about Trina Schart Hyman's character from this short section?

   Suggest that someone read her autobiography and find events in her life that have influenced her illustration of children's books. Ask for a volunteer to check out her *Little Red Riding Hood* (Holiday House, 1983) from the school or public library. That student should show Hyman's illustrations to the class and describe Hyman's early love of the story. Did the student like the fact that *Self-Portrait* was an autobiography and that the author did her own illustrations for it? Why or why not?

6. Introduce Gloria Kamen's biography *Kipling, Storyteller of East and West* by asking the class if anyone has ever heard of Mowgli or of any of the *Just So Stories,* such as "The Elephant's Child." Suggest that a class member read Kamen's biography and one of Rudyard Kipling's *Just So Stories.* If available select the one illustrated by Nicolas (Doubleday, 1912, 1952). Ask that person to share with the class Kipling's character traits, events that influenced his writing, why he wrote the *Just So Stories,* and a brief summary of the plot of the story read.

7. Introduce Jean Little's autobiography *Little by Little* by telling the class that this is the true story of a nearly blind girl who became an author. Her eyes appeared crossed and she suffered ridicule and rejection from other children. Why? She found great happiness in books and became a teacher and writer of children's books. What do they suppose her first published book was about?

   Suggest that someone read the autobiography and share with the class Jean Little's character traits, the obstacles she overcame, and the reasons the book keeps one reading. The author's note tells whether the book is authentic or fictionalized. Justify her decision.

Ask someone else to check out Little's *Mine for Keeps* (Little, Brown, 1962) from the school or public library and share its plot after the author report. Why did Little choose to write about a girl like Sally? In what ways was Sally like Jean Little?

8. Introduce Bill Peet's autobiography by showing the illustrations and asking the class if anyone remembers reading any of his books. Have some from the school library to show the class. Tell them he started to draw during his boyhood in Grandview, Indiana. Illustrating books was his first boyhood ambition. His work at Disney Studios also influenced his work.

Ask someone in the class to read the autobiography and share his boyhood experiences, his work at Disney Studios, and how he set about writing *Hubert's Hair-Raising Adventures,* his first children's book. What in Peet's style keeps one reading his autobiography?

9. Introduce Robert Quackenbush's *Mark Twain? What Kind of Name Is That?* by asking whether anyone in the class has heard of Tom Sawyer. Let the class recall anything they know about Twain's *The Adventures of Tom Sawyer.* Suggest that someone read Quackenbush's biography *Mark Twain? What Kind of Name Is That?* and report to the class the events in Twain's life that influenced his writing career. Discuss with the class the elements of style that keep the reader interested in the biography. What character traits of Twain are revealed by Quackenbush?

10. Introduce James Stevenson's *When I Was Nine* and *Higher on the Door.* Tell the class that these two books are recollections by Stevenson, now a grandfather, of life in the 1930s. Ask two students to read the two books and decide what elements of style make the books enjoyable. Have them locate and read at least one of Stevenson's books from the school library. Does anything about the style of his stories remind the students of his autobiographies?

If either of the students know a man over sixty-five years old, interview that person and ask for recollections of when that person was a child. What did he do for enjoyment? Did he ever take a trip? If so, where and how did he go? Become a biographer and write the recollections in a paragraph to share with the class.

11. Introduce Margot Zemach's *Self-Portrait* by telling the class that Margot Zemach won the Caldecott Medal for her illustrations in her husband Harve Zemach's *Duffy and the Devil* (Farrar, Straus & Giroux, 1973). Get the book from the school library to show the class. Read the note about the illustrations at the back of Zemach's *Self-Portrait* that refer to *Duffy and the Devil.* Read the note on page 27 and show the illustration.

Suggest that a class member read Zemach's autobiography and a book illustrated by her. Report to the class on Zemach's character traits that were revealed in her autobiography and the reason she illustrated certain children's books. Did the illustrations from her books included in *Self-Portrait* add to its appeal for the reader?

FOLLOW-UP ACTIVITIES FOR INDIVIDUALS OR SMALL GROUPS:

1. Read Clyde Robert Bulla's *A Grain of Wheat.* Write a short paragraph telling why he gave the book that title.
2. Read Gloria Kamen's biography *Kipling, Storyteller of East and West.* Notice the titles of the chapters. Select any two and write a paragraph about why those titles were appropriate.
3. Jean Little said that a series of lectures by Virginia Sorensen, the winner of the Newbery Medal for *Miracles on Maple Hill* in 1957, was very helpful to her. Read Sorensen's *Miracles on Maple Hill* (Harcourt Brace Jovanovich, 1956). Write a paragraph telling whether its style and plot deserved for the author the Newbery Medal. Justify your answer. It was written in 1956. Will young people enjoy it today? Why or why not?
4. After hearing a report on Jean Little or reading her autobiography *Little by Little,* check out from the school library one of Jean Little's fiction books, such as *Different Dragons* (Viking, 1987), *Lost and Found* (Viking, 1986), or *Mama's Going to Buy You a Mockingbird* (Viking, 1985). Read the book and share the plot with the class, or write a paragraph about why Jean Little was able to write this book. What events in her own life prepared her?
5. Read James Stevenson's two autobiographies *Higher on the Door* and *When I Was Nine.* If you were going to publish a weekly neighborhood newspaper, how would you duplicate it? Design a front page and write the headlines for stories from your neighborhood.

Enjoying Modern Fantasy

STUDENT OBJECTIVES:

1. List the fantasy elements of a story.
2. Give ways the author made the story seem believable.
3. Compare two fantasies by the same author to find common elements.
4. Identify the theme and relate it to life today.
5. Create a fantasy.
6. Create a newspaper story about a fantasy character.

RECOMMENDED READING:

Cleary, Beverly. *The Mouse and the Motorcycle.* Illustrated by Louis Darling. William Morrow, 1965. (Objectives 1, 3)
   Ralph Mouse borrows Keith's toy motorcycle and gets to keep it, after finding an aspirin to help Keith feel better.

Howe, Deborah and James. *Bunnicula.* Illustrated by Alan Daniel. Atheneum, 1979. (Objectives 1, 2, 3, 6)
   Chester, the cat, gets into trouble with the family as he tries to warn them that the bunny they found is a vampire.

Juster, Norton. *The Phantom Tollbooth.* Illustrated by Jules Feiffer. Random House, 1961. (Objectives 1, 2, 4, 6)
   Milo goes through the tollbooth and takes an imaginary journey into a land where words become very important.

Karl, Jean E. *Beloved Benjamin Is Waiting.* E. P. Dutton, 1978. (Objectives 1, 2, 6)
   After her mother disappears, Lucinda, fearful of a gang, hides in an abandoned caretaker's house in a cemetery where she is contacted by alien beings through a statue of Benjamin.

Kendall, Carol. *The Gammage Cup.* Illustrated by Erik Blegvad. Harcourt Brace Jovanovich, 1959, 1988. paper. (Objectives 2, 4)
   In the land of the Minnipins the rebellious few who refuse to conform are exiled but later save their people from the ancient enemies.

Langton, Jane. *The Fledgling.* Harper & Row, 1980. (Objective 4)
   A young girl's desire to fly is satisfied when she is befriended by a Canadian goose.

Lewis, C. S. *The Lion, the Witch and the Wardrobe.* Illustrated by Pauline Baynes. Macmillan, 1950, 1988. (Objectives 1, 2, 4)
Four children walk through the wardrobe of a house where they are visiting and enter Narnia, a cold wintery land under the spell of the white witch.

Norton, Mary. *The Borrowers.* Illustrated by Beth and Joe Krush. Harcourt Brace Jovanovich, 1953. (Objectives 1, 2, 3)
A tiny family lives below the floor of a house in England and borrows from the humans upstairs.

Seldon, George. *The Cricket in Times Square.* Illustrated by Garth Williams. Farrar, Straus & Giroux, 1960. (Objectives 1, 3, 6)
Chester, the cricket, saves the Bellini's newsstand in the Times Square subway station by giving nightly concerts.

Steig, William. *Abel's Island.* Farrar, Straus & Giroux, 1976. (Objectives 4, 6)
The mouse Abel spends a year alone on an island after he is swept away by torrential rain when he tries to retrieve his bride's lost scarf.

Van Allsburg, Chris. *The Mysteries of Harris Burdick.* Houghton Mifflin, 1984. (Objective 5)
Fourteen illustrations steeped in mystery with a suspenseful title and first line for each provide impetus for creating an imaginary plot.

Van Allsburg, Chris. *The Stranger.* Houghton Mifflin, 1986. (Objectives 1, 2, 4, 6)
A mysterious figure, perhaps Jack Frost, stays with the family of the farmer whose truck accidentally struck him until he must leave so the seasons can change.

Winthrop, Elizabeth. *The Castle in the Attic.* Illustrated by Trina Schart Hyman. Holiday House, 1985. (Objectives 4, 6)
William's live-in baby-sitter decides to go back to England, and because he lacks confidence, William uses a dangerous charm to make her stay.

GROUP INTRODUCTORY ACTIVITY:

Preparing for the Activity: Locate Chris Van Allsburg's *The Stranger.* For the extending activity, be sure that students have writing materials. Have a blackboard or overhead available.

Focus: Ask the students if anyone can tell you what a fantasy is. Why would the child who told his mom that a gorilla spilled his glass of milk be inventing a fantasy? Help the students think of events, characters, and ideas that would make a fantasy. Write *Fantasy* on the blackboard or overhead and list the characteristics that the class has identified. Ask leading questions as needed.

Objective: This activity is designed to satisfy the objectives of listing the fantasy elements, giving ways the author makes the story believable, identifying the theme and relating it to life, and creating a newspaper article about a fantasy character. Tell the students that you will read a fantasy to them, and that you need them to keep track of the fantastic elements in the story—those things that cannot really be or happen. Tell them that you also want them to note the ways the author works to keep his story believable and realistic.

Guided Activity: Introduce Van Allsburg's *The Stranger* by telling the students that Chris Van Allsburg writes and illustrates his books, so that the illustrations often carry plot elements that are not present in the words. Read the story once, and ask the students to tell you who the stranger is, and how they know this. They may name him Jack Frost, the Spirit of Winter, etc. Ask when in the story they first thought that the stranger might be the element of fantasy in the story. Collect the clues that the students remember that led them to this idea and write them on the board. Now reread the story, this time asking the students to be prepared to enlarge on the list and find the more subtle clues that Van Allsburg has left for them. Add to the list. Ask the students to decide which of these clues are fantastic elements. They should decide that almost all of them are.

Explore how Van Allsburg's setting and characters make this fantasy believable. Find details in the illustrations that give the story realism. Ask the students if they think the words or the illustrations carry most of the fantasy. Which adds most of the realism?

Ask the students to identify a theme for the story. What may Van Allsburg be saying about nature and scientific information about why the seasons change? Does he seem to accept science as the only answer to the reason that seasons change?

Extending Activity: With the students discussing in small groups, ask the group how this story would be different if it were being reported by the local newspaper. How would a reporter explain the fantasy and the magic? Could a reporter explain it? Let the students discuss how a newspaper reporter could solve the problems of the fantasy in this story. Now ask the groups to work together and write a short newspaper story based on *The Stranger*. They might report on the fact that Farmer Bailey's land stayed green longer than the land around it and offer explanations. They could report on the visitor that the Baileys have staying with them. They could interview the Baileys or their neighbors. Remind the students that they will want to write first paragraphs that include "who-what-where-and-when" information. You could have students read examples of newspaper articles as models for their work. Share and display the students' articles, saving all work to be included in a class newspaper at the end of the fantasy unit.

Van Allsburg is an author who may be well known to students. Ask for volunteers to read or reread three of his other books and hold a book discussion about how Van Allsburg handles fantasy in his books. Have them search for differences and similarities among the books.

FOLLOW-UP ACTIVITIES FOR TEACHER AND STUDENTS TO SHARE:

1. Introduce Deborah and James Howe's *Bunnicula* by reading Chapter 1. Then have the class discuss what situations have been introduced that make the story seem believable. What fantasy elements have been introduced thus far? Ask a small group (perhaps a reading group) to complete the story for a group discussion. After each member of the group has completed the book, discuss the fantastic elements introduced into the story. Characterize Chester and Harold. Is the group satisfied with the ending of the story? What might have been another possible ending? Ask a member of the group to write a news story about the family's finding Bunnicula.

2. Introduce Norton Juster's *The Phantom Tollbooth* by reading the first chapter. Ask the class if they have ever felt like Milo. If so, that should make the story seem believable to this point. Tell the class that the story is a fantasy that focuses on words, and after you read each day, the class will play with words in some way. Read Chapter 2. Then ask the class to think of an expectation they have for the future. Ask each to write a short paragraph describing that expectation and how they will get beyond it.

    After reading Chapter 3 "Welcome to Dictionopolis" to the class, divide them into groups of five and have them think of a sentence that includes a word for which the others can suggest synonyms. Ask them to write the sentence at the top of a paper, roll the top down as if it were a scroll, and pass the paper on to the next person to add a synonym. Afterwards, share the scroll with the class.

    After reading aloud Chapter 4, "Confusion in the Market-place," have everyone in the class think of a word they would buy that would have special use, and have them justify the purchase. Acquire a book of quotations from the library and ask a different class member to pick a quotation to place on the blackboard each day that the book is read.

    After reading Chapter 7, "The Royal Banquet," have everyone think up a half-baked idea to share with the class. After reading Chapter 9, "It's All in How You Look at Things," have each class member think of something they see one way but their parents see another way because of their differing points of view. (For example, the child wants to watch a late movie on a school night but the parents say he/she must go to bed and get a good night's sleep.)

After reading Chapter 10, "A Colorful Symphony," have everyone write a short paragraph justifying the instrument each of them would select to play at sunrise. After Chapter 12, "The Silent Valley," let the class discuss what they would miss most if there were no sound. After Chapter 14, "The Dodecakedrow Lead the Way," have committees of children make road signs to nearby towns, including miles, rods, yards, etc. After Chapter 16, "A Very Dirty Bird," let the class discuss what differences there would be in their town or city if everyone lived in ignorance.

After Chapter 18, "Castles in the Air," let the children discuss a possible theme for the book that was given by Rhyme and Reason. After completing the book have the class identify the real and fantasy elements of the story. What had Milo learned that is important for everyone to consider? Many more ideas will be inspired by reading the book. After appropriate chapters, children can be asked to make up "gross exaggerations," "threadbare excuses," etc. Be sure to ask a class member to volunteer to write a news story for this book that will be a part of the fantasy newspaper.

3. Introduce Jean Karl's *Beloved Benjamin Is Waiting* by telling the class that Lucinda Gratz, the protagonist, is afraid. Her big brother Joel is going away to school. Her parents fight all the time and she could get hurt. In addition, she has a neighborhood gang to fear. Home is not safe, but where can she go? Let the class discuss whether this sounds like fantasy or contemporary realistic fiction and why.

   Ahead of time ask a boy and a girl to practice reading the conversation of Joel and Lucinda that makes up the chapter "Before." Ask them to make a script of the lines of the two characters and read it to the class. Then let the class discuss why the chapter was titled "Before" when no others are named. Ask that those who are interested read the book and do a suggested individual activity.

4. Introduce Carol Kendall's *The Gammage Cup* by telling the class that in this story, set in the land of the Minnipens, there was a "best village" contest with the Gammage Cup to go to the winner. In a town meeting at Slipper-on-the-Water it was decided that in order to win the contest all villagers must wear green and their homes should be painted green. If the class lived in that village, would they want to abide by this decision? Why or why not? Muggles and her companions refused. What does the class think will happen to them?

   Ask someone to read the book and tell the class what Muggles and her companions did—and how they became heroes.

That person should also explain the theme of the book, how it applies to today's world, and what situations made the fantasy seem believable.

5. Introduce Jane Langton's *The Fledgling* by reading the two-page first chapter "The Present." Have the class guess what the present was. Does anyone know anything about Walden Pond, where the present was found? Ask for a volunteer to go to the library and find out facts about Walden Pond and Thoreau to share with the class. Ask someone else to read the book and share its plot and theme. After the two people report, let the class decide why Walden Pond was an appropriate setting for this story. Is the theme applicable to today's young people?

6. Introduce C. S. Lewis' *The Lion, the Witch and the Wardrobe* by telling the class that Lucy is one of four children visiting the house of an old professor. Lucy steps through a wardrobe and meets Fawn in a strange land. Ahead of time ask a member of the class to go over Lucy's lines in the first three pages of Chapter 2, "What Lucy Found." With the teacher reading Fawn's lines, share those pages with the class as if it were the script of a play. Why does the class suppose it has been winter for a long time in Narnia?

   Ask someone in the class to read the story and share the plot briefly with the class. Have them identify a theme and tell how it applies to today. What are the fantasy elements of the story? What did the author do in Chapter 1 to make the story seem believable?

7. Introduce Mary Norton's *The Borrowers* by reading Chapter 1. Ask the class how Mary Norton made the story seem believable. What things are constantly lost in the houses of class members? Why was the book named *The Borrowers?* Ask that someone read the book and share with the class the unique character traits of Homily, of Pod, and of Arrietty. In what ways do they remind the reader of humans? What are the fantastic elements in the story? Kate and the reader could almost believe the story, but what did Mrs. May say on the last page to make the reader question whether the borrowers really existed?

8. Ask two children to read George Seldon's *The Cricket in Times Square.* Ask them to share it with the class as if one of them were a newspaper reporter interviewing the other, Chester the cricket, on how he arrived in New York City and how he saved the Bellini family from bankruptcy. Let the class discuss the fantasy elements revealed in the interview. Remind the two students who read the book to develop a short newspaper article about Chester's concerts.

9. Introduce Chris Van Allsburg's *The Mysteries of Harris Burdick* by describing to the class how Van Allsburg says the publishing house acquired the pictures. Show the pictures and read the titles and first lines. Let the class select one picture and as a

group develop a plot line for a fantasy based on that title and first line. Then ask each member of the class to examine the book, select a title and first line, and write a short fantasy using that beginning. Have them read their stories aloud to the class if time allows.

10. Introduce Elizabeth Winthrop's *The Castle in the Attic* by telling the class that it is the story of a ten-year-old gymnast who lacks self-confidence. After a fantastic, dangerous journey to rescue a friend he has wronged, he gains the confidence he needs. Ask for a volunteer to read the book and briefly summarize the plot and identify the theme for the class. Someone else may want to read the book and write a newspaper article about how this talented gymnast gained confidence.

FOLLOW-UP ACTIVITIES FOR INDIVIDUALS AND SMALL GROUPS:

1. Read Beverly Cleary's *The Mouse and the Motorcycle.* Write a paragraph about the fantasy elements of the story.
2. Read Beverly Cleary's *The Mouse and the Motorcycle.* Write the paragraph Keith's teacher will request about his summer vacation.
3. Read Beverly Cleary's *The Mouse and the Motorcycle.* Find one of two sequels, Cleary's *Ralph S. Mouse* (William Morrow, 1982) or Cleary's *Runaway Ralph* (William Morrow, 1970) at the school or public library. Write a paragraph comparing the fantasy elements in the two stories. How were they alike? Was Ralph's character different in any way in the two stories?
4. Read Deborah and James Howe's *Bunnicula* and James Howe's *The Celery Stalks at Midnight* (Atheneum, 1983). Write a paragraph describing the similarities in the fantasy elements and in the style of the two books.
5. Read Jean Karl's *Beloved Benjamin Is Waiting.* Write a paragraph describing what you think is the most fantastic element of the plot.
6. Read Jean Karl's *Beloved Benjamin Is Waiting.* Draw a picture of Lucinda reading aloud to Benjamin in the caretaker's house or another scene that appeals to you. Caption the picture.
7. Read Jean Karl's *Beloved Benjamin Is Waiting.* Write a human interest newspaper story about Lucinda's happiness in her new foster home.
8. Read Mary Norton's *The Borrowers* and one of the sequels. Write a paragraph describing the commonalities in style and fantasy elements found in the two stories
9. Read George Seldon's *The Cricket in Times Square.* Then read Seldon's *Tucker's Countryside* (Farrar, Straus & Giroux, 1969). List the fantasy elements that both stories have in common.

10. Read William Steig's *Abel's Island.* List a theme of the story and tell how it applies today. Write a newspaper article and headline describing Abel's return.

Introducing Classics

STUDENT OBJECTIVES:

1. Identify the theme and decide whether it is relevant to today's young people.
2. Characterize the protagonist and justify decisions with descriptions or events from the book.
3. Assess elements of style and decide whether the book will keep young people reading today.
4. Compare old and new editions of classics to see which format is most appealing.
5. Share in play form scenes from a classic.
6. Identify characters in children's books that were written over seventy-five years ago.
7. Determine why specific picture books written over fifty years ago have become classics.

RECOMMENDED READING:

Barrie, J. M. *Peter Pan.* Illustrated by Jan Ormerod. Viking, 1988. (Objectives 1, 2, 5, 6)
Wendy, John, and Michael fly with Peter Pan to Never Never Land where they have many exciting adventures.

Baum, L. Frank. *The Wizard of Oz.* Illustrated by Michael Hague. Holt, Rinehart & Winston, 1982. (Objective 5)
Recounts the adventures of Dorothy and her friends, the Tin Woodman, the Scarecrow, and the Cowardly Lion as they find out the truth about the Wizard.

Brunhoff, Jean de. *The Story of Babar, the Little Elephant.* Random House, 1933. (Objective 7)
The story of an orphaned elephant who runs away from the jungle and lives for a time with a lady in Paris.

Burnett, Frances Hodgson. *The Secret Garden.* Illustrated by Shirley Hughes. Viking, 1988. (Objectives 2, 4, 5, 6)
Colin's health is restored as he and his cousin secretly reclaim the lost garden.

Carroll, Lewis. *Alice's Adventures in Wonderland.* Illustrated by Anthony Browne. Alfred A. Knopf, 1988. (Objectives 4, 5, 6)
Colorful illustrations add to the humor of the tale of the little girl who falls down a rabbit hole and meets many strange characters.

Collodi, Carlo. *The Adventures of Pinocchio.* Illustrated by Roberto Innocenti. Alfred A. Knopf, 1988. (Objectives 1, 2, 4, 6)
Italy's streets and countryside are illustrated in this classic story of the mischievous wooden puppet who wants to be a real boy.

Dickens, Charles. *A Christmas Carol.* Illustrated by Lisbeth Zwerger. Picture Book Studio, 1988. (Objectives 2, 3, 4, 5)
Illustrations add to the story of the miser who learns the true meaning of Christmas when he is visited by three ghosts bringing visions of his past, present, and future.

Flack, Marjorie. *Angus and the Ducks.* Doubleday, 1930. (Objective 7)
A Scotch terrier puppy gets into difficulty while satisfying his curiosity.

Grahame, Kenneth. *The Wind in the Willows.* Illustrated by Michael Hague. Henry Holt, 1980. (Objectives 1, 2, 5, 6)
Water Rat, Toad, Badger, and Mole share a special friendship and unique adventures.

Howe, John. *Rip Van Winkle.* Little, Brown, 1989. (Objectives 1, 2, 3, 5, 6)
Striking illustrations help to recapture the mood of Washington Irving's famous tale.

Leaf, Munro. *The Story of Ferdinand.* Illustrated by Robert Lawson. Viking, 1936. (Objective 7)
A sensitive bull in Spain would rather smell the flowers than fight.

Milne, A. A. *The World of Pooh; the Complete Winnie-the-Pooh and The House at Pooh Corner.* Illustrated by E. H. Shepard. E. P. Dutton, 1957. (Objective 5)
Two titles in one recount the adventures of Christopher Robin and his friends.

Seuss, Dr. *And to Think That I Saw It on Mulberry Street.* Vanguard, 1937. (Objective 7)
Imaginative rhyme tells the tale of Marco's reaction to the horse and wagon he sees on Mulberry Street.

Spyri, Johanna. *Heidi.* Illustrated by Ruth Sanderson. Alfred A. Knopf, 1984. (Objectives 1, 2, 3, 6)
An illustrated version of the story of the Swiss orphan who leaves her grandfather and their mountain home to help an invalid city girl.

Twain, Mark. *The Adventures of Tom Sawyer*. Illustrated by Ted
Lewin. Simon & Schuster, 1982. (Objectives 2, 4, 5, 6)
Tom's pranks cause Aunt Polly great concern.

GROUP INTRODUCTORY ACTIVITY:

Preparing for the Activity: Locate John Howe's retelling of Washington Irving's *Rip Van Winkle*.

Focus: Explain to the students that a classic story is one that was
written long ago for a different audience but continues to be read by
modern people because of some elements in the story that still make
it interesting. If an author lived in the 1880s, what would the students expect him to write about? *Not* to write about? What would be
the biggest difference between this author's stories and a modern
author's stories? How have people probably changed and not changed
during this time?

Objective: This lesson is designed to satisfy the objectives of identifying the theme and deciding if it is relevant, characterizing the protagonist and justifying the decisions, assessing elements of style,
deciding whether the book will keep today's young people reading,
identifying characters in children's books that were written in the
nineteenth century, and sharing scenes from a classic. Tell the students that you will read a modern version of a classic tale by
Washington Irving, the author who wrote *The Legend of Sleepy
Hollow*. Tell them to note the details that prove that this story was
set in the 1700s in what is now New York. Tell them that you will
ask them to tell you which elements of the story still have a meaning
to us today, and which elements are now hard to understand because
of the differences in setting.

Guided Activity: Introduce Howe's version of *Rip Van Winkle*. Tell
them that this story was first written in 1819. Read the note about
the author on the dust cover that explains Howe's interest in period
costumes. Ask the students to take careful notice of the costumes of
the characters. Tell them that there are three different periods of
clothing represented in the story.

Read the book, giving the students time to study the illustrations.
Ask the class to give you a possible theme of this story and to explain
why this story has continued to be popular for over one hundred
years. Could their themes be relevant and meaningful in today's life?

Ask the students to characterize Rip. Is he a dynamic character?
Some may say that he does not change his actions even though he
ages. Is he a well-rounded character? Ask the students to think of
some of Rip's decisions. How does he act at home? In the village? In
the Catskills with the strange little men? What do Rip's decisions tell

about him? Why would the children of the village enjoy being with him? Why does his wife get so angry at him?

Reread some of the descriptive passages, and ask the students if this is a style that authors use today. Have the students find examples of imagery in the story.

Ask if the students identified the three different costume styles—the clothing of Hudson and his crew, Rip's clothing, and the costumes of the people in the village twenty years later. What important historical event has Rip slept through? Ask the students to tell you how they know this.

Extending Activity: Divide the class into three or four groups to work on recreating scenes from the book. Ask the students to use their imagination to fill in some of the things that could have been said or done by the characters. Suggest that the scenes in the Catskills, in the village twenty years later, and in the village at the beginning of the story would be scenes that would include action and dialogue. Ask the students to write their scenes and to act them out for their classmates. Comment on the scenes, and keep the scripts so that some can be included for the parent program.

FOLLOW-UP ACTIVITIES FOR TEACHER AND STUDENTS TO SHARE:

1. Introduce J. M. Barrie's *Peter Pan* by telling the students it was first published in 1911; their great-grandparents may have read it. However, this is a new edition illustrated by Jan Ormerod. How many students know who Peter Pan was? How did they learn about the story? Have the class try to recall the story of Peter Pan.

   Then read the first chapter. Have the class characterize Mrs. Darling. Would they like to have their mothers rummaging through their minds at night? Why or why not? Point out the lines about Mrs. Darling's "kiss." What is the meaning?

   Does the story begin as they thought it would? If they were reading the story, do they suppose they would continue reading after the first chapter? Why or why not? Tell the students that there is much more conversation later in the story.

   Ask two students to read the story and make a script to read of the scene between Peter and Wendy in Chapter 3, "Come Away, Come Away." Begin when Wendy asks Peter why he is crying and continue to the end of the chapter. Have them read their scene to the class. Is this chapter more appealing than the first chapter? Why or why not? Ask the two students to tell the rest of the story, continuing to be Peter and Wendy as they share the telling of the plot. Identify a theme for the story and justify the decision.

2. Introduce L. Frank Baum's *The Wizard of Oz* by asking the class if they have ever heard of the Yellow Brick Road or the Cowardly Lion. In what classic are they found? After the class responds, tell them that Baum's *The Wizard of Oz* was first published in 1900 as *The Wonderful Wizard of Oz*. Ask two people to read the story and to introduce it to the class by writing a script of the conversation when Dorothy meets the Scarecrow, saves him, and they set off on the Yellow Brick Road.

3. Introduce Frances Burnett's *The Secret Garden* illustrated by Shirley Hughes by telling the class that although this is a 1988 edition, the book was first published in England in 1911. Share Chapter 1 and Chapter 2 up to the scene on the train when Mary and Mrs. Medlock are on their way to London.

   Ahead of time ask someone to read the part of Mary on the train while the teacher reads Mrs. Medlock. Omit the description and complete the chapter with the conversation only. Have the class characterize Mary, justifying their decision from what the author said or Mary did. Does the class sympathize with her? What do they think will happen to her?

   Ask a member of the class to volunteer to complete the story and summarize the plot for the class. Ask that person to identify and justify a theme. Perhaps someone else will want to complete the book and together they can read aloud the lines when Mary finds Colin in Chapter 8, "I am Colin." Begin with Colin's lines asking Mary if she is a ghost. Finish the scene when Colin wants to show her what is behind the silk curtain.

4. Introduce Lewis Carroll's *Alice's Adventures in Wonderland* by telling the class that Lewis Carroll, whose real name was Charles Dodgson, was a professor of mathematics at Oxford University. He never married and his hobbies were mathematical puzzles and photography. He loved children and often took the three daughters of Dr. Henry Liddell on picnics. One day he began to tell them the "Alice" stories. Later he made the stories into a book for children, *Alice's Adventures in Wonderland* illustrated by John Tenniel. Try to find an edition with the original illustrations to show the class so they can compare and contrast the format with the modern version illustrated by Anthony Browne.

   Ask the children what they know about Alice. If anyone knows the story, ask them where they heard it. Read Chapter 1, "Down the Rabbit-Hole." Let the class characterize Alice. If this were a realistic story instead of a fantasy, would Alice drink the liquid in the bottle?

   Ask two children to read the story. Ask them to make the conversation in Chapter 5, "Advice from a Caterpillar," into a script and read Alice's and the caterpillar's discussion to the class. Also have them briefly share the entire plot. Be sure to have them describe other characters such as the Mad Hatter and the Queen of Hearts. What in the plot and style makes the story be called a humorous fantasy?

5. Introduce Carlo Collodi's *The Adventures of Pinocchio* by telling the class that the original edition of the book was published in 1892. Read Chapters 1, 2, and 3 aloud, showing the class Innocenti's striking illustrations. When you finish reading the last sentence in Chapter 3, "What happened afterward is almost too much to believe and I shall tell you about it in the following chapters," ask the class to suggest why the author closed the chapter with that sentence. After reading the chapters, let the class discuss the characters of Geppetto and Pinocchio. Will Pinocchio change? If so, what do they think will cause him to do so?

   Ask someone to read the book and share Pinocchio's adventures with the class. Did he change and thus become a dynamic character? What is the theme of the book? Is it relevant today?

6. Introduce Charles Dickens' *A Christmas Carol* by telling the class it was first written in 1843. Ask the class how many have heard of Scrooge. How do they know of him?

   Before reading Stave One "Marley's Ghost" up to the scene where the nephew arrives, tell the class that in this portion there is no conversation and that Dickens characterizes Scrooge. Have them listen for the figurative language that is an important element of the style, and for character traits of Scrooge. After that portion is read, let the class share the figurative language they heard, such as "solitary as an oyster" and "tight-fisted hand at the grindstone." Talk about the meaning. Characterize Scrooge.

   Ask three students to read the story and make a scene into a script to read to the class. The conversation between Scrooge, his nephew, and the clerk that follows the portion read by the teacher is a good scene to share. Ask these students to summarize the plot and to justify that Scrooge is a dynamic character—a character who changes over the course of the tale. Have the class find other editions of the story for a display. After examining them, the class can decide which edition is more appealing to the reader.

7. Introduce Kenneth Grahame's *The Wind in the Willows* by telling the class that Grahame was a banker who lived in England. He entertained his only son by telling him stories about Toad, Water Rat, Mole, and Badger. Later these stories were developed into a book *The Wind in the Willows* published in 1908. Tell the class that one of the best-remembered chapters in the book is Chapter 2, "The Open Road." Read the chapter. Have the class characterize Toad. Then have them recreate the conversation, recall the events, and play out the scene.

Suggest that someone read the book and share the animals' adventures with the class. Do the class members believe that Toad is a dynamic character who was changed forever? What is a theme for the book?

8. Introduce Munro Leaf's *The Story of Ferdinand* by asking the class how many remember the story. After they recall it as best they can, tell the class that after you read the story, written in 1936, you are going to ask them to justify why today's children will or will not like it. After the story is read and the class has discussed its popularity, tell them that an expression often heard is that someone likes "to sit just quietly and smell the flowers." What is meant by this expression?

   Show the class Marjorie Flack's *Angus and the Ducks,* written in 1940; Jean de Brunhoff's *The Story of Babar,* translated from the French in 1933; and Dr. Seuss's *And to Think I Saw It on Mulberry Street,* written in 1937. Ask members of the class who wish to do so to practice reading aloud any one of the stories. After the student has read the story aloud to the teacher, he or she should learn how to hold the book so the audience can see the illustrations. Then the teacher may want to arrange for the student to read the book to a group of children in kindergarten or first grade. Have the student discuss with the younger children why they liked or did not enjoy the book. Ask the students to report their findings back to their own class.

9. Introduce A. A. Milne's *The World of Pooh* by telling the class that this is two stories in one, *Winnie-the-Pooh* and *The House at Pooh Corner,* written by an English author in 1926 and 1928. These books were written when Milne's son Christopher was small, and the stories were inspired by Christopher and his toys.

   Ask the class how many have heard of Winnie-the-Pooh. How many have read the book or heard it read? If more say they have heard of Winnie-the-Pooh than have read the book, ask them the source of their information. If it is the Disney movie, explain that the Disney film studio took many liberties with Milne's story as they made it into a film.

   Read the class one of the more familiar chapters such as "In Which Piglet is Entirely Surrounded by Water." After reading the chapter have the class recall the action and dialogue in order to act out the scenes. Use different students in each segment of the chapter so that many are involved as actors as well as listeners. Suggest that members of the class may want to read the book and play out other scenes for the class.

10. Introduce Johanna Spyri's *Heidi* illustrated by Ruth Sanderson by telling the class that the setting of the story is Switzerland and that the story was first published in 1880. Ask the class if anyone knows the story of Heidi. If so, where did they hear it?

    Show the class Ruth Sanderson's illustrations and the format of the book. Does the book look like one they would select to read? Read the first chapter of *Heidi,* "The Alm-Uncle." Will readers enjoy the style? Suggest that someone read the book and briefly talk about the plot, Heidi's character traits, and a theme for the book. Does the theme apply to young people today?

11. Introduce Mark Twain's *The Adventures of Tom Sawyer* by telling the class that the author's name is really Samuel Clemens and that he lived as a boy in Hannibal, Missouri, the setting of the story. The story closely resembles incidents that happened to Twain and his friends. Ask if anyone has visited Hannibal and seen Twain's home, stood by the statue of Tom Sawyer and Huck Finn, and gone through the cave that was the setting for the chapter when Becky Thatcher and Tom Sawyer were lost. *The Adventures of Tom Sawyer* was first published in 1876.

   Read to the class the famous scene in Chapter 2 when Tom is whitewashing the fence. Explain to the class that Aunt Polly told Tom to whitewash thirty yards of fence that was nine feet high. He soon tired of his task and persuaded his friend Jim to help. Aunt Polly caught them and Tom had to begin whitewashing again while Jim went flying down the street to get water.

   Begin reading the scene as Tom gets out all the things from his pocket to see if he can buy his freedom. Read the remainder of the chapter. Have the class characterize Tom. Let the class review the incidents in the scene, recall the conversation, and have the class act out the story. Suggest that two people may wish to read the story and summarize the plot for the class. They may want to make a script for the conversation between Aunt Polly and Tom after the boys returned home from the island, and read it to the class.

   Suggest that the class ask grandparents or older people if they read *The Adventures of Tom Sawyer* when they were young. What do they remember about the plot of the story? Ask the students to report their findings to the class. If old editions of the story are available at students' homes or the library, ask the students to set up a display.

12. At the close of the unit let the class plan a parent program using the scripts developed by the students as a basis for the event's activities.

FOLLOW-UP ACTIVITIES FOR INDIVIDUALS OR SMALL GROUPS:

1. Read J. M. Barrie's *Peter Pan* illustrated by Jan Ormerod. Try to find another edition of the story in the school or public library. Compare the two editions. Which would appeal most to today's reader? Find the copyright date of the editions you are comparing. Share the books and your report with the class.

2. Read J. M. Barrie's *Peter Pan* illustrated by Jan Ormerod. Take it home to share with your mother or father. Does he or she remember reading *Peter Pan* as a child? Was the edition read by your parent as appealing as this one? Report the answer to the class.

3. Read J. M. Barrie's *Peter Pan* illustrated by Jan Ormerod. Write a paragraph describing Wendy's character traits, justifying your decisions with events from the book.

4. Read Frances Burnett's *The Secret Garden* illustrated by Shirley Hughes. Try to find an older woman who remembers reading *The Secret Garden* as a child. What does she remember about the plot? Help her recreate it. Report to the class what she remembered. Find other editions of *The Secret Garden* in the school or public library. Show them to the class so they can compare the format and illustrations in various editions. Which do they prefer? Why?

5. Read Lewis Carroll's *Alice's Adventures in Wonderland* illustrated by Anthony Browne. Select your favorite poem in the book. Practice reading it aloud and then share it with the class.

6. Read Carlo Collodi's *The Adventures of Pinocchio* illustrated by Roberto Innocenti. Find other editions of the book and write a paragraph justifying which edition you would recommend that children read.

7. Read Carlo Collodi's *The Adventures of Pinocchio* illustrated by Roberto Innocenti. Now reexamine the illustrations and write a paragraph justifying how three specific illustrations extended your understanding of the setting or plot.

8. Read Kenneth Grahame's *The Wind in the Willows*. Draw an illustration of your favorite scene and write a short paragraph describing it.

9. Read Kenneth Grahame's *The Wind in the Willows*. Write a paragraph defending whether the book would keep young people reading it today.

10. Plan a Pooh Program in which members of the class will play scenes from the Winnie-the-Pooh stories for a third grade class. Be sure to include some Pooh and Christopher Robin poems. Perhaps a parent will agree to make honey cakes to serve after the program.

11. After sharing Washington Irving's *Rip Van Winkle* illustrated by John Howe, read another version of the same story. Report to the class the differences in the two versions and which you think will appeal most to students today.

12. After hearing Washington Irving's *Rip Van Winkle* read in class, do research on the Catskill Mountains, Washington Irving, or Henry Hudson's contribution to American History. Share your research with the class.

Using Information Books

STUDENT OBJECTIVES:

1. Determine whether the information is up-to-date and accurate.
2. Assess the clarity of directions in a "how-to-do-it" book.
3. Determine whether style, format, and illustrations help to hold the reader's interest.
4. Identify the aids that help the reader to understand the book, to look up specific topics, or to locate further information.
5. Determine whether the reader is given information indicating the author's expertise.

RECOMMENDED READING:

Arnosky, Jim. *Sketching Outdoors in Autumn.* Lothrop, Lee & Shepard, 1988. (Objectives 3, 5)
   Many familiar autumn subjects for sketching are included with techniques for capturing the essence of the scene.

Cooper, Kay. *Where Did You Get Those Eyes?* Illustrated by Anthony Accardo. Walker, 1988. (Objectives 2, 3, 4)
   The reader who wishes to research his or her family tree is given concrete suggestions for organizing facts, interviewing, and locating information.

Cooper, Michael. *Racing Sled Dogs.* Clarion, 1988. (Objectives 3, 4)
   After introducing the Iditarod and the first woman winner, Cooper narrates history of sled dog racing and describes how dogs are trained.

George, Jean Craighead. *One Day in the Prairie.* Illustrated by Bob Marshall. Thomas Y. Crowell, 1986. (Objectives 3, 4, 5)
   The animals in an Oklahoma wildlife refuge sense an approaching storm and prepare for it.

Gryski, Camilla. *Super String Games.* Illustrated by Tom Sankey. William Morrow, 1987. (Objectives 2, 5)
   Gives step-by-step directions for string games originating in lands around the world.

Hautzig, Esther. *Make It Special.* Illustrated by Martha Weston. Macmillan, 1986. (Objective 2)
   Includes instructions for making cards, decorations, and small gifts.

Hobson, Burton. *Stamp Collecting as a Hobby.* Sterling, 1986. (Objectives 2, 4)
Explains how to begin collecting and describes the types of stamps available.

Lauber, Patricia. *The News about Dinosaurs.* Bradbury, 1989. (Objectives 1, 2, 4)
Presents new scientific thinking that replaces earlier theories about dinosaurs.

Mango, Karin N. *Codes, Ciphers and Other Secrets.* Franklin Watts, 1988. (Objectives 2, 4)
Discusses why codes are prepared and gives ideas for making and breaking them.

Patent, Dorothy. *A Horse of a Different Color.* Illustrated by William Muñoz. Dodd, Mead, 1988. (Objectives 1, 3, 4)
Introduces the colors and markings that are characteristic of a variety of horse breeds.

Sullivan, George. *All about Baseball.* G. P. Putnam's Sons, 1989. (Objectives 1, 4)
Gives basic information about the game and about the major league teams.

Tessendorf, K.C. *Barnstormers and Daredevils.* Atheneum, 1988. (Objectives 3, 4, 5)
Relates the history of barnstorming and describes the exploits of pilots who were stunt fliers in the 1920s.

GROUP INTRODUCTORY ACTIVITY:

Preparing for the Activity: Locate *The News about Dinosaurs* by Patricia Lauber. Prepare a bulletin board with the title *The News Is,* to be used for the extending activity. Have drawing and writing materials available for the extending activity. For the extending activity, collect a number of books about space and space travel from the library. Make sure that there is a range of copyright dates, including the oldest books that the library owns. Books may need to be borrowed from the public library or other schools.

Focus: Ask the students if they can think of a field of knowledge that is changing very quickly, where information is always new. Lead them to think of space technology, computers, older biographies about living or recently deceased people, information about developing countries, and sports events where records are being broken. Now, ask them if it would be important to them, if they were reading a book on one of these subjects, to be reading an up-to-date book. How can they tell if a book is up-to-date? How can they check the information in a nonfiction book to be certain that the facts are accurate and recent? How can a reader discover if the author of a book is an expert whose knowledge is to be trusted? How important is it to a reader to know about the author? Help the class think of checking copyright dates, examining information at the beginning and end of the books for facts about the author, and reading the book jacket information.

Objective: This activity is designed to satisfy the objectives of determining whether the information is up-to-date; determining whether style, format, and illustrations hold interest; and determining whether the reader is given any information about the author's expertise. Ask the students to think for a moment about dinosaurs and prehistoric animals. Do they think that this is an area where new discoveries would be made often? Should the information in a book about dinosaurs always be up-to-date and accurate? Brainstorm to discover what the class already knows about dinosaurs. You may wish to have one of the students write the facts on the chalkboard. Ask if anyone is aware of any new discoveries about dinosaurs. Tell them that you will read several pages in a new book about dinosaurs that makes many of the other books inaccurate and out of date. Ask them to listen for new facts that are different from the commonly accepted information.

Guided Activity: Read pages 7, 16, 22–25, and 32 in Patricia Lauber's *The News about Dinosaurs.* Point out the pronunciation guide at the beginning of the book, the pattern that Lauber uses to present the accepted information, and then the more accurate recent information. Ask the students to share the new information that was the most interesting or startling to them. Tell them that Lauber's book uses the format of "The News Is" to present many new facts about the dinosaurs.

Ask the students if they could think of some way to find out if the author is an expert in this area. Lead them to the acknowledgments and the book jacket information about Lauber. Read the information about the artists. How does this lead the reader to accept the information as accurate?

Discuss the patterned format of the book: Does it help the students understand the book? Why or why not? Do the illustrations add to the effect of the book? Have students explain. Is the information on the page laid out attractively with enough white space between lines so the book seems readable?

Extending Activity: Using the space books collected, ask the students if they would expect all these books to contain accurate, up-to-date information. Have them think of some of the reasons for differences in facts within the books. Divide the class into groups, and give each group a number of the books. Ask them to compare information and facts among the books. Have them try to find a recent book that contradicts an older one because of advances in knowledge. Ask them to contrast the copyright dates, and to decide on the most accurate and least accurate book in their group. Ask them to be ready to share with the class differences in facts and information, and to justify their decisions about the expertise of the authors. Have each group explain their findings to the class, and then have the class decide on the most accurate book of the entire group.

Find information in one of the oldest, and one of the most recent books that could be written in the same pattern that Lauber used, in which the older information is written before the new. Have each group write two paragraphs from their books, using the words, "The news is" and display their work on the bulletin board of the same title.

During this unit, whenever a student finds new information on any subject that can be written in this same format, have him or her add two paragraphs to the bulletin board, including the sources and the student's name.

Ask volunteers to read the rest of *The News about Dinosaurs* and report to the class some of the other facts that Lauber included in the book. Have the volunteers rewrite these facts for the bulletin board.

FOLLOW-UP ACTIVITIES FOR TEACHER AND STUDENTS TO SHARE:

1. Introduce Jim Arnosky's *Sketching Outdoors in Autumn* by asking the class: What scenes or objects in nature does autumn bring to mind? Before reading a portion of Arnosky's book, ask the class to listen both for the story of each sketch and the techniques for making it. Ask them to notice any descriptions that will help them characterize Arnosky.

   Read the book through page 21, in which the fox's hole and catch is sketched. Then, sharing the pictures again, let the class discuss specific facts related to the choice of scene and the drawing techniques identified. Would they like to know Arnosky? Why? Do they feel he has expertise in drawing? Did his style of writing, his sketches, and the format of the book keep them interested? Why or why not?

   Urge the children who are interested to complete the book and sketch something they see outdoors in nature that is typical of the season. Ask them to share their sketch with the class, describing any techniques of sketching they used which were suggested by Arnosky. Make a bulletin board display of the students' drawings under the title "Sketching Outdoors."

2. Introduce Kay Cooper's *Where Did You Get Those Eyes?* by asking the students if anyone in their families has ever traced the family tree. Why do people do that? Read Chapter 1 and ask again for reasons why people trace the family's history.

Show the class the family tree chart on page 15 and the parent interview questions on page 16. Ask someone who is interested to read the book and to fill in their own family tree chart. Decide whether the directions given for tracing one's ancestry are clear. Is the book written in a readable style? What value is The Directory as a reader's aid? Ask the student to share ideas about the book's use with the class.

If a number of students are interested in tracing their family trees, ask a local member of a historical society to visit the class to talk about techniques and problems in searching for information. Place a map of the United States on the wall and ask students to place small pennants on it showing where parents and grandparents were born. Post their genealogical charts on a bulletin board. Have them add a family picture to their tree if one is available.

3. Introduce Michael Cooper's *Racing Sled Dogs* by asking how many have heard of the Iditarod. Read Chapter 1, which describes how Libby Riddles won the Iditarod race, the first woman to do so. Let the class discuss the dangers she faced. Did the style of writing keep one interested?

   Ask someone to read the book and share with the class facts about the care and training of dogs for racing.

4. Introduce Jean George's *One Day in the Prairie* by reading the dedication and the information about the author on the book jacket. Ask what made Jean George qualified to write this book. Why did she include a bibliography?

   Tell the class that George's writing style includes a great deal of figurative language. Ask them to listen for figurative language as you read the first four pages. Read to the class and then let them identify the figurative language they heard. Did it help them picture the setting? How would the class feel if they were alone there with a storm approaching?

   Suggest that someone read the book and report on what happened to Henry, Red Dog, and the other animals that day. How did George make the day memorable for the reader?

5. Introduce Camilla Gryski's *Super String Games* by reading the introduction, reading the directions for one game, and demonstrating to the class how it is done. Read to the class the book cover's description of Gryski. Can one feel she is an expert on the subject?

   Ask interested members of the class to read directions for other games and demonstrate to the class. After several have shared, ask them to decide whether the directions were clear and easy to follow.

6. Introduce Burton Hobson's *Stamp Collecting as a Hobby* by reading the Introduction and Chapter 1, "Stamps Bring the World to Your Door." Ask the class why stamp collecting is a popular hobby. Is there someone in the class who collects

stamps or who wants to begin a collection? If so, ask that person to read the book and decide on its value for the collector. Does it have a readable style and appealing format? Why is the list of newspapers and magazines to which one can subscribe an aid worth including in the book? Do the acknowledgments make the reader feel the author is qualified to write the book?

If no one is a stamp collector but the class is interested, invite someone from the local post office to talk about beginning a collection. Urge children with other types of hobbies to select a book from the library on that hobby and assess its writing style and value. Is the "How to begin" information useful? If the library or hall has a display case, arrange for the children to display their hobbies for others to enjoy.

7. Introduce Karin Mango's *Codes, Ciphers and Other Secrets* by reading aloud Chapter 2, "Keeping Secrets in the Past." Then read Chapter 4 "Secret Ciphers" and pages 70 and 71, "Making Up Secret Languages." With these suggestions for ways to develop secret messages as background, urge pairs of students to read sections of the book and, following directions, develop a secret message to share with the class. Decide whether the book provided clear instructions.

8. Introduce Dorothy Patent's *A Horse of a Different Color* by covering the text below the photos of several horses and seeing if anyone can identify them. Urge someone who likes horses to read the book in order to share interesting facts with the class, determine if the style and format is pleasing, and identify the value of the glossary to readers. If the reader doubts the accuracy of any fact in the book, how can he or she check the accuracy?

9. Introduce George Sullivan's *All about Baseball* by showing the class the list of "All-Time Major League Leaders" at the back of the book. Ask the class why one must check the copyright date before being sure the list is accurate.

Ask someone in the class who is a baseball fan or player to read the book. Ask that person to share with the class some interesting new information he or she found. For whom would the list of "Baseball Words and Terms" be an aid?

10. Introduce K.C. Tessendorf's *Barnstormers and Daredevils* by reading Slats Rogers' introduction and Chapter 1. How would a farmer react today if a plane landed in his field? Would the pilot be likely to have only twenty cents in his pocket and have to figure out a way to get gasoline?

Did the class enjoy the writing style? How do they think Tessendorf knows about situations such as this? Read "K.C. Tessendorf Writes" on the jacket of the book.

Call attention to the bibliography and notes. Why are they included? Ask someone in the class to read the book and share interesting information about barnstormers in general.

FOLLOW-UP ACTIVITIES FOR INDIVIDUALS OR SMALL GROUPS:

1. Read the rest of Michael Cooper's *Racing Sled Dogs* after the teacher introduces it. Notice the list titled "For More Information." Write to one of the addresses to obtain information about dog racing in that state.
2. Read Jean George's *One Day in the Prairie*. Suppose she planned to write a book about a wildlife refuge or park in your state. List special natural features she would need to include.
3. Select an item from Esther Hautzig's *Make It Special* to make. Create the item and show it to the class, describing how you made it and indicating whether you found the directions to be clear and easy to follow.
4. Use the list "For Further Reading" in Karin Mango's *Codes, Ciphers and Other Secrets* to locate additional books in the library on the subject. Read one and share a secret code with the class.
5. Read Dorothy Patent's *A Horse of a Different Color*. Select three facts, and by using two additional library sources, check the accuracy of those statements.
6. With a friend read the sections on Charles Lindbergh and on Wiley Post in K. C. Tessendorf's *Barnstormers and Daredevils*. Use the library to find out what happened later to both of those men. Pretending to be Wiley Post and Charles Lindbergh, tell the class about your barnstorming experiences and your later life.

Appendix A: Glossary

Autobiography A book about a person's life written by that person.

Backdrop setting Place and time of the action; not essential to the development of characters, action, or theme.

Biography A work based on facts about a person's life written by someone else.

Caldecott Medal Award given annually by the Association for Library Services to Children, a division of the American Library Association, to the illustrator of the most distinguished picture book for children published in the United States the previous year. The illustrator must be a citizen or resident of the United States. Established in 1938, the award is in honor of Randolph Caldecott, nineteenth-century illustrator of children's books.

Character Any person, animal, or personified object that assumes a role in a story.

Characterize To identify the traits of a character in a literary work.

Choral reading Oral reading or reciting of poetry in which two or more readers speak in unison.

Classic A literary work that has survived for generations because of its quality and appeal to readers.

Climax An important experience, decision, or discovery of the main character that is the turning point in a story.

Colloquial language Informal local or regional expressions in conversation.

Compare To discover and explain how objects or ideas are alike.

Concrete poetry A poem, the written lines of which form a shape related to the content of the poem.

Conflict Struggle between a character and self, nature, society, or another character.

Contemporary realistic fiction Creative imaginative literature that reflects the complications of modern life.

Contrast To discover and explain how objects or ideas are different.

Couplet A verse of poetry made up of two consecutive lines that rhyme.

Cumulative story A literary pattern that repeats details and builds on them to make a progressively longer story. *The House That Jack Built* is an example.

Dewey Classification Numerical categorization of topics by which materials are arranged in a library.

Dynamic character A character who changes within a story, usually by maturing. Such a character can be described with the pattern "at the beginning of the story he/she was...; but at the end of the story he/she was . . . ."

Falling action Events within a story that occur after the climax and lead to the story's resolution.

Fantasy A work in which imaginary, unreal, or magical elements are combined to present a universal truth.

Figurative language An inventive, fresh use of words to create a new way of experiencing something familiar, often through a sensory image; a nonliteral use of language to appeal to the imagination.

First person point of view The narrative perspective in which the one telling the story knows only his or her own thoughts but can report the actions of all other characters.

Flat character A character within a story who is described by few details, seems one-dimensional, and may be a minor character.

Foreshadowing Clues provided to help the reader predict the outcome and avoid disbelief.

Format General makeup of a publication, including its size and shape, layout of the pages, white space between lines, quality of paper, and arrangement of illustrations.

Free verse A poem that has no rhyme and uses strong unpatterned rhythm.

Genre A distinctive type or style of literature in which books have similarities.

Haiku An ancient Japanese poetic form, usually having seventeen syllables divided among three lines. The first line of the poem has five syllables; the second, seven; and the third, five. A haiku often describes a season or animal, and it expresses a thought, feeling, or mood.

Integral setting Place and/or time are essential to the development of characters, action, or theme.

Limerick A five-line nonsense poem. The first and second lines rhyme, and the third and fourth lines rhyme. The last line usually picks up the rhyme from line 1.

Limited omniscient point of view Third person perspective in which the narrator knows the thoughts and actions of one character or at times a very few characters.

Mood Predominant emotion or feeling conveyed in a work of literature.

Mystery A suspense story in which the protagonist must solve a baffling situation by using clues.

Narrative poetry Poetry that tells a story and has elements of plot.

Narrator The person who is telling the story, not always a character *in* the story.

Newbery Medal Award given annually by the Association for Library Services to Children, a division of the American Library Association, to the author of the most distinguished book for children published in the United States during the previous year. The author must be a citizen or resident of the United States. Established in 1922, the award is named in honor of John Newbery, an eighteenth-century British publisher and bookseller.

Omniscient point of view Third person perspective in which the narrator of a story knows the thoughts and actions of all the characters.

Parody An imitation of a known work written in the same style keeping the form and sequence of the original but changing words and names.

Patterns in literature Literary style that uses language to repeat words or build images in a manner that makes the work highly predictable.

Phonics The relationship between letters and their sounds. Basal reading series identify and sequence these sounds and present lessons to establish beginning readers' skills in recognizing letter–sound correspondence.

Plot The events in sequence within a story including rising action, climax, falling action, and resolution.

Point of view The perspective from which a story is written.

Prediction Using background information and past experiences to anticipate upcoming events. In reading, this skill engages students' abilities of observation and helps create a purpose for reading.

Problem and solution Simple introduction to plot with "problem" standing for introduction and rising action, and "solution" standing for climax, falling action, and resolution which lets young children discuss conflict in terms that have meaning to them.

Protagonist The main character in a work.

Psycholinguistics Interdisciplinary field that combines psychology and linguistics to describe how readers process print. Includes interactive models of reading, miscue analysis, and deep structure comprehension.

Repetitive story Literary pattern in which key phrases, words, or sentences are repeated within the story in a predictable manner.

Resolution The last element of plot when conflicts and problems are solved and remaining questions are answered.

Rhyme Repeating sounds at the ends of words, usually recognizable in poetry.

Rhythm Also called *meter* in poetry, it depends on arranging words so their accented and unaccented syllables form repetitive patterns of sound.

Rising action A sequence of events presenting the conflicts and complications that lead to the climax.

Round character A well-developed character within a story who is described with many details and traits.

Sequel A book that continues the story of the characters introduced in an earlier work. Characters' actions are sufficiently consistent with their earlier development so that readers can predict their actions and feelings in the sequel.

Sequence Succession of events within a narrative. Sequence should be logical and recognizable.

Setting The place and time in which the action of a literary work occurs.

Sound imagery Details that describe pitch, tone, loudness, or softness of sounds. Such details help the reader imagine the sounds described.

Static character A character within a story who shows no change of traits by the climax of the story.

Strategies in reading Plans readers can learn that allow them to recognize situations and patterns in order to build meanings from the author's words.

Style An author's unique way of combining the literary elements.

Symbol A person, place, or thing, that stands for something else by reason of relationship to it and thus conveys two levels of meaning.

Theme The meaning or unifying truth(s) of a literary work.

Transitional A grade designed for young children who are developmentally young or not academically ready for first grade. Children study a specialized curriculum giving practice in school behavior, beginning reading, and mathematics concepts.

Visual imagery Details that describe the size, color, shape, and position of an object to make the reader imagine the sight in a vivid manner.

Visual literacy Vision skills that when developed allow people to integrate sensory experiences, interpret objects and symbols, and communicate with others about subjects seen in the environment or viewed in illustrations.

Whole language A teaching strategy that incorporates reading and writing by students in meaningful contexts. Language is the means to communicate and not the purpose for study alone. Comprehension is the goal of readers; expression of meaning is the goal of writers.

Appendix B: Sources for Reading and Children's Literature Theory and Techniques

Anderson, Gordon S. *A Whole Language Approach to Reading.* Latham, MD: University Press of America, 1984.
   Introduces language theories and gives suggestions for instruction and evaluation in classrooms using the whole language approach.

Bauer, Caroline Feller. *This Way to Books.* New York: H. W. Wilson, 1983.
   Gives techniques for book talks, storytelling, poetry sharing, and a variety of language arts activities.

Bloom, Benjamin, ed. *The Taxonomy of Educational Objectives. Handbook I. Cognitive Domain.* New York: Longmans, Green, 1956.
   Groups thinking skills by levels to assist educators in making decisions about curriculum.

Goodman, Kenneth. *What's Whole in Whole Language?* Portsmouth, NH: Heinemann, 1986.
   Describes development of oral and written language abilities and presents a whole language instructional model.

Holdaway, Don. *Stability and Change in Literacy Learning.* Exeter, NH: Heinemann Educational Books, 1984.
   Summarizes current research in literacy with suggestions for making literacy development natural and successful.

Huck, Charlotte S. *Children's Literature in the Elementary School.* 4th ed. New York: Holt, Rinehart & Winston, 1987.
   Surveys children's literature and the literary elements to be included in a literature-based reading program.

Laughlin, Mildred Knight, and Letty S. Watt. *Developing Learning Skills Through Children's Literature.* Phoenix, AZ: Oryx Press, 1986.
   Introduces author and subject units by grade level for use in a literature or reading program.

Lukens, Rebecca. *A Critical Handbook of Children's Literature.* 4th ed. Glenview, IL: Scott, Foresman, 1990.
Presents literary devices for training children to make critical judgments about literature.

Sloan, Glenna Davis. *The Child as Critic.* 2nd ed. New York: Columbia Teachers College Press, 1984.
Presents a theoretical framework for teaching literary criticism to children.

Smith, Frank. *Essays into Literacy, Selected Papers and Some Afterthoughts.* Exeter, NH: Heinemann Educational Books, 1983.
"Twelve Easy Ways to Make Reading Difficult" and other essays show the development of Smith's reading theories.

Smith, Frank. *Reading.* 2nd ed. Cambridge, England: Cambridge University Press, 1985.
Discusses in detail theories and issues in language development and the reading process.

Trelease, Jim. *The Read-Aloud Handbook.* New York: Penguin, 1985.
Strongly justifies reading aloud to children.

The WEB: Wonderfully Exciting Books. Columbus, OH: The Reading Center, Ohio State University.
This periodical includes reviews of childrens' books and presents a "web" of activities to extend a single book or genre.

Index

Compiled by Linda Webster

This index contains authors, illustrators, and titles of books and nonprint media, as well as subjects.

MILDRED KNIGHT LAUGHLIN

Mildred Knight Laughlin is a professor in the School of Library and Information Studies at the University of Oklahoma. She, with Letty Watt, is the author of *Developing Learning Skills Through Children's Literature: An Idea Book for K–5 Classrooms and Libraries* (Oryx Press, 1986). She has a B.A. in English from Fort Hays State University, Hays, Kansas; an M.A. in Education from Wichita State University, Wichita, Kansas; and an M.L.S. and a Ph.D. in Education from the University of Oklahoma, Norman, Oklahoma.

CLAUDIA LISMAN SWISHER

Claudia Lisman Swisher is an English and reading teacher at West Mid-High School, Norman, Oklahoma. She is a graduate of Indiana University, with a B.S. in English education and an M.S. in reading education. She studied special education at the University of Iowa. Mrs. Swisher worked for eight years as an elementary reading teacher. She has also served as an elementary librarian and as a special education resource room teacher.